Job 32:18
By
ADRYANN GLENN

For Mustard Seed Ministries

EM Street Books LLC

Copyright © 2012 by Adryann Glenn

www.emstreetbooks.com

All rights reserved.
This book or parts thereof may not be reproduced in any form, without prior written consent of the publisher, except in brief quotes used in reviews.

EM Street Books LLC
ISBN-13:978-0615784038
ISBN-10:0615784038

*In memory of
Evelyn "Gram" Law*

Dedicated To:
"Him & Her" (See you when I get there)

Acknowledgments

First and foremost, all praise and worship to the Father I thank You for choosing me, revealing Your truths to me, equipping me, holding on to me, and most importantly for the love extended through the sacrifice of your Son.

Danielle: In more ways than I feel you'll ever know, in more ways than I could ever show... this is a reflection of us.

Mom: Your example and prayers molded me. Thank you for life, tough love, and never letting me give up.

Jayson, Tammy, "Skeedabutt", and "Robbe": A man couldn't ask for better brothers and sisters. Thanks for the love, support, and keeping me humble. "Phatman, "B.B.", Leah: Uncle "Max" loves you! I pray you all avoid the pitfalls, and embrace the blessings. "Alley Cat" & Elijah: you didn't think I'd forget about you... I'm always here for y'all, Love ya! Ms. Tina, Brit Brat, J.J., Mr & Mrs. Layne y'all are family! Love ya, love ya, love ya!

Before I go on, if you're my family... then you know there's a lot of us. If you're my family... whether or not you're on this list doesn't change that. Uncle Mark (and his whole clan); My late Uncle Wilbur (and his clan)' Grip, Percy, Donald, Tracy (and that ever-growing clan!); Seth & Rico; What up!; Aunt Diane (and her clan); Aunt Gloria (and her clan); Aunt Jean (and all y'all); Aunt Liz (and all y'all); Aunt Lori (and all y'all); Uncle Beezy (and all y'all); Lori & Terri (and all y'all); Aunt Carol, Court', and Eddie; Byron (and all y'all)

My church families: Heritage Fellowship, Wayman Chapel A.M.E., Reconciliation, City of Refuge.

My mentors and surrogate mothers: Ms. Anita (thanks for teaching me how to use my true voice); Rev. Ruth Harvey; Kim & Kelly (y'all taught me praise & worship); Mike

Howard; Mr. & Mrs. (Min.) Parker; The Church ladies(Ms. Lucille, Ms. Roberta, Ms. Baltrop, Mrs. Toatley, Mrs. Edwards, Ms. Sharon, Kathy, Vickie, Ms. Bonita, Mrs. Walker); Mr. Jeffers (ALWAYS in my corner); Phyllis Arnold (unfinished business); Chaplain Bob Milne (keep living in the Spirit); Chaplain Ray Perez; Chaplain Chuck Freer (my brother, soon we'll fellowship); Deacon Duane (oh, soon and very soon); Big Brother Cassius & Jeff (didn't think I'd forget you!); KiJuan (let's do it)

<u>Loved ones:</u> The whole Dulles Park; 10-2-7 (AITE!); Six-One-Deuce (My N.S.U. fam); Frontline; 2ya Bop (Are there words to describe how we do, ALWAYS); Ash Di Dog (You and Mom mean the world to me); NikNak (keep pushing, keep loving); Trish (you are <u>sooooo</u> wise, thanks for being you); Kit Kat (pens don't bite, do you have paper allergies, LOL....love ya); Manda Mami (nobody knows what we share, hopefully one day they'll be blessed to know something similar); Peanut (last nite...uh uh, uh uh); Felicia (you didn't think I'd forget you); Zolania/Z. Wigs (SURPRISE!!); Brandon (Dirty District); B. Mo (you my favorite ___ ___); Brother Abe (You saw and believed in me before I did, LOVE YOU); The Aleem Family; Jen Brader (you were there when the world left me in the cold); Rolston (live up to your last name! Love you Bruh!); Corey & Josh Thomas; Ab "da Butcher" (You already know!?!); Big D (How 'bout' dem Cowboys?); Erk (a brother, big homie, thanks for <u>always</u> holding me down); Alex Kumah (you inspire me); The Davenport's (don't believe the hype, never that); P. Ray; Ali Zaidan (I love you brother, just didn't know how to appreciate you); "D. Dot" Young; "E.Bone", Meghan Carr, "Damnwell" Webb, "Uncle" Morrie; all the fellaz and ladies from Heritage Youth group growing up (always in my heart)

<u>Brother In Chains</u>: Wesley Pinckney, David Tapscott, Kenyon Majors, "T", Torris, Frank, Travis, "Concordance"

Chris, Hector, Russ, Aaron, Jerz, Derek Renforth (YO!); Cain Lewis, Mark, "Izzy", "Hi-Way," Philly Rob (No Cheez-Wiz), Matthew Painter, Mc Crickard, Mikey, Moss, Big Rome, Man-Man, J Black, Boo-Boo, Mr. A (get at me), "Uncle" Bo (love ya), Jack, Marvin, "The Neddle", Jimbo, Sesay, Jack (how the floors?), Dale Arrington (know I'm praying for ya'), Solo (what, thought you wouldn't be here?), J.Turner (let's get it!), Tucker, Ol' School, T.I., Tim, Vic, Chalk, Danny, Jay, Mike A, Sean (Norfolk State to the State Pen, my man!), Lil G, Black (Craig), Toby, The State Fair Crew (May May, Star, CardiCardi, Fox, Sizzax, Bay, Midget, House, Dustin), T. Atkins, Ghost, Big' Quise, "Silk Jones, Keith, Paul, Braaah-zil, Rod, and of course B.G. (He's trying to work in you, let Him)

The readers, ya'll make it worthwhile. I love each of you....pray for me...

Last, but most importantly....Q! Thanks for always being REAL, and this opportunity. This just the start, ya dig? Love you bruh bruh. Stay a "hunnid"...

If I forgot you, I'll get you next go around. This is just the beginning... Be Blessed Be Faithful

VIII

"Lord God bless me with the faith of Abraham, the humility of Moses, the zeal of Jacob and Phinehas, the fearlessness of Joshua and Caleb, the heart of David, the wisdom of Solomon, the favor of Daniel and Joseph, the boldness of Stephen, the obedience of angels, and the anointing of Jesus."

AMEN

Job 32:18

BLOW THE TRUMPET

"When you go to war in your land against the enemy who oppresses you, then you shall sound an alarm with the trumpets, and you will be remembered before the Lord your God, and you will be saved from your enemies."
(Numbers 10:9 NKJV)

Brothers and sisters, I come to you today with a message I feel is long overdue. Oh, this subject is past over due, and something must be done immediately. Some of you have Lo-jack, and Viper security systems on your car; ADT and Brinks to protect your home; passwords to protect your computer and email; pin numbers for your bank accounts. We live in a society that is obsessed with security, and we are constantly bombarded with the newest updated ways to alert us when our protection has been breached. I don't want anyone to take me out of context; there is nothing wrong with taking the necessary precautions in these days and times. Why it would be foolish given the current trends in society to do anything other than that. Yet, why do we spend such little time protecting the things that really matter? The Lord has placed this message on my heart, so if I step on a few toes take it to the Lord in prayer, AMEN?

Please turn in your bible to Numbers 10. Here in verse 2 we find God instructing Moses to construct two silver trumpets. These instruments are to be used in order to direct the tribes of Israel. It goes on to give specific instructions for how the trumpets should be blown to instruct the tribes of Israel. For instance; when both trumpets are blown the congregation is to gather at the entrance of the tabernacle. If one is blown then only the leaders of each division are to meet with Moses, so forth and so on. It is said in verse 8, **_"The sons of Aaron, the priests, shall blow the trumpets; and these shall be to you as an ordinance_**

forever throughout your generations." This is telling us that when it is time to alarm God's people, then the "priests" are to blow the trumpets. Take note this responsibility has been laid on a specific group of people, the "clergy" so to speak. It also says that ***"these shall be to you as an ordinance forever throughout your generations.***" This means that God still intends for us to adhere to this protocol. I direct this to all Ministers, Reverends, Pastors, Bishops, and leaders throughout the Church specifically. **Jeremiah 3:15(NKJV)** says; ***"And I will give you shepherds according to My heart, who will feed you with knowledge and understanding."*** This means that you have a divine appointment in the Kingdom to tend to our Father's flock. Therefore it is your responsibility to defend this flock, to guide this flock, to see to their overall well being. When you see something going wrong, it is your job to speak up and "blow the trumpets." Often we don't want to hurt people's feelings, or risk the stability afforded us by our position....so we do more harm to the Kingdom then good. We put ourselves, and our interests, before those of our Father. This hurts God's people and makes them vulnerable to attack. Oh.... I know it's wonderful when people walk up and congratulate you on such a good sermon, or when you're recognized by all the good "Christian organizations" for your work. Yet whose accolades are you supposed to be concerned with, man or God's? Sound the trumpets in your congregations today, do the work that you've been appointed and anointed to do.

This brings us to verse 9, bear with me as we take this text statement by statement, and analyze it. ***"When you go to war in your land against the enemy who oppresses you"***. Would you agree that we as Christians are in a war of this very nature today? If you look at the current climate of today's culture, you can see we are behind enemy lines. There are far too many of our Father's commands being overlooked, and compromised. It's acceptable today to have children out of wedlock, live with members of the other sex out of wedlock, be openly defiant to parents, party and drink to excess. Not only are these and many aspects of our culture deemed "acceptable,' they are even promoted on many levels. Day by day, more and more of our Christian values are demonized. It is to the point where us as Christians are no longer allowed to openly witness about our faith....it that isn't enemy oppression then I don't know what is.

The next part of the scripture reads, ***"then you shall sound an alarm with the trumpets"***. I tell you today my brothers and sisters; this is what we ought to be doing. If you agree with my previous description of our current situation, then you must also agree with God's plan of action. I challenge you today to sound the trumpets in your homes, offices, churches, towns, states, countries, Let the children of God be gathered and prepared for war. We have no problem answering the call when it's time for the church picnic, let's be just as adamant to answer this call to arms. Throughout the world today let the trumpets sound, May God's faithful come together....as He has instructed us to do. If sounding the alarm means you have to walk off that job.....then I advise you do as such. If sounding that alarm means you have to confront the leadership of your churches.....then I advise you do as such. If sounding the alarm means you have to throw away all the music, TV's, video games, and other devices to reclaim your children....then I advise you do as such. If sounding the alarm means you need to walk away from that relationship you're in.....then I advise you do as such. If sounding the alarm means you need to do some serious self inventories (and it probably will).....then I advise you do as such. Sound the alarm my brothers and sisters, sound the alarm now!

God knows it won't be easy, He knew our lives would be in this predicament. I know many of you are sitting there today saying; "I can't just walk away from the life I'm living. Oh, how will I survive? How will people look at me? How can I have victory, when the whole world is against me? What's the use in me making a difference, when nobody else wants to?" The reason is simple: **_"and you will be remembered before the Lord your God"_**, When we follow God's instructions as His children ought to, he will recognize us as His children. This is just an example of what is meant by separating yourself from the world. If you're doing the same things the un-repented are, how can you still consider yourself a "child of God"? So don't be afraid to stand up against the wrongs of this world. Boldly announce to the world through your words and actions that you are going to stand for God. He will see you, and He will remember you. One day He's coming back, be sure that you are remembered. The scripture ends by saying, _**"and you will be saved from your enemies"**_. Though it seems as though we are outnumbered, He will still give us the victory. We must hold on to His promises, we must be obedient to what He has commanded us. I know it gets hard; I deal with the same issues as you all. But you have to hold on. He is a faithful God, and He has already won victory over the enemy. _**"We are hard pressed on every side, yet not crushed; we are perplexed, but not in despair; persecuted, but not forsaken; struck down, but not destroyed..."**_ (2 Corinthians 4:8-9 NKJV). I tell you today, the victory is yours. Although you might not be able to see it, you have to know it's there. Hold on to this passage in 2 Corinthians as you sound the trumpets in your life. When people tell you that your crazy, or wrong ...... you tell them to refer to Romans 8:37 (NKJV) _**"Yet in all these things we are more than conquerors through Him who loved us"**_. Stay in His will, abide by His commandments, walk in His ways, and blow the trumpets as He has instructed.

Today my brothers and sisters I pray for fearlessness, wisdom, strength, discernment, trust, faith, love, and all necessary tools needed for us to have victory in this war. Don't give the enemy anymore time to strengthen His grip on our people, and communities. BLOW THE TRUMPETS!!!!!!

BE BLESSED BE FAITHFUL

Job 32:18

#1110672 & #09-00494

"Therefore whoever hears these saying of Mine, and does them, I will liken him to a wise man who built his house on the rock: and the rain descended, the floods came, and the winds blew and beat on that house; and it did not fall, for it was founded on the rock. But everyone who hears these saying of Mine, and does not do them, will be like a foolish man who built his house on the sand: and the rain descended, the floods came, and the winds blew and beat on that house; and it fell. And great was its fall."
(Matthew 7:24-27 NKJV)

Brothers and sisters, is it okay if I'm transparent today? Is it okay if I tell my story? The Father put this message on my heart sometime ago, yet hadn't given me the words to properly convey the message. How many of you know sometimes He wants us to meditate on our blessings from time to time? Sometimes we need to remember where He's brought us from, to understand the magnitude of His favor, and love in our personal lives. **AMEN!!!** As I sit here and listen to J. Moss and Anthony Hamilton sing "I'm Not Perfect" I realize that God has provided the ideal conditions for His message to be brought forth. I believe it **is** of paramount importance that those of us who spread God's word tell others our testimony. It keeps us humble, and people are more receptive when they know the person speaking to them can relate.

In June of 2010 the storms of life began beating on my life. To be totally honest, the storm had been raging for years. In order to give you the full scope of the storm, I must start at the beginning. August of 1997 I left home to go to Norfolk State University (BEHOLD THE GREEN AND GOLD!!!!). On that day there were so many ideas I had about my life. The Lord had performed a miracle just by providing the necessary funds for me to pursue a college degree. The morning I left I had just attended church, received a powerful message from Rev. Tate, as well as words of encouragement from my church family. I specifically remember Mr. Parker saying, "A lot of people will try to get you off your goal....stay focused." My mind was focused on the Lord and his purpose for my life. Then I got to school, and in the midst of my focus on everything but God the grey skies began to come in my life. **_"But everyone who hears these sayings of mine, and does not do them, will be like a foolish man who built his house on the sand..."_** Within a month I was concentrating on everything but my studies. See, Satan has a million tricks to get you off the path God has placed you on. At the time my life was all about making hip-hop music. At the time the Tidewater Area was putting out many well known acts....Missy Elliott, Timbaland, The Neptune's, Nicole Wray, The Clipse, and many others. It seemed like wherever I went I was running in to someone who could help me pursue my goal. Suddenly homework time turned in to cipher time. Instead of consulting and learning from my professors, I was studying the entertainment industry with producers. I had begun smoking marijuana a number of years before leaving home, but my use greatly increased. All the while I was making great strides in music, yet I was not fulfilling the true purpose and calling on my life. I began to build my life around these aspirations of being a "superstar." I had turned away from that which I had been instilled within me. Instead of building on the "solid rock" of the Gospel, I began building on the "shifting sands" of society. I always find it ironic that I was living in the Tidewater region, which as many of you know is near the beach, I'm here to tell you that; "YES, God does have a sense of humor."

What most people dispel as myth is that the entertainment industry comes with a lot more than music and singing. There is a large criminal element, and I found myself very "capable" of prospering in such an industry. Soon I traded in the books and pens, for scales and 'packs." Just so no one is confused, we're still talking about my first semester of college. Yet, God always provides a way for us to get back on the right track. He blessed me with wonderful professors, who were not naive to life's temptations. I was given a "modified" learning platform because they felt as though I was wasting my God given talents and they didn't want to see me "go down the tubes, "Instead of seeing the blessing I was being given at the time, I attributed it to my superior talent for manipulation. LOL!

That Spring I came home, seasoned and a totally different person than had left just eight months previous. I wasn't home a month before I went back to Hampton to visit my roommate. Andre and I had been through it all, and in many ways were closer than brothers. That weekend he introduced me to a manager who was working with two of our other friends who also rapped. Once he gave us his credentials, I performed an impromptu audition and exchanged numbers. I left and came home the next day, not thinking much of it. The following Saturday I received a call from the manager saying he was in the area, and he'd like to meet up with me. We had a bite to eat, then he offered to bring me back to Hampton so we could work on my career. Without hesitation I went home, packed a bag, woke up my Father.....and I was off!!!

On the way down we got a call from Andre, who was having some issues, and quickly decided he would be moving in with us. In my heart I felt as though things couldn't have been better, oh how little did I know. Long story short, we had a great summer, made some great music, yet everything ended up turning sour. The next school year started and I spent more time hustling and rapping, then studying and attending class. At the end of the school year I came home, and found myself in a predicament. Instead of handing the problem like a man, I ran on back to Norfolk feeling like the "gingerbread man". Notice I said, I ran back to Norfolk....not school. At this point I was going to school part time; my full time occupations were hustling, rapping, and womanizing. One day my friend J.J. called and told me there was a warrant for my arrest, and the police in Herndon were searching for me. I dismissed the severity of the situation. Went home for the holidays, stayed low, and was back in Hampton for New Year's. I went through the second semester of that year having a ball. On another note there were some family problems going on, and instead of running to the Father....I submerged myself more in the streets.

When summer break came I decided to go home and see if I could save some money, maybe help Mom out in any way possible. One night while sitting on the fence out front an officer rolls up out of nowhere and asks, "Are you Adryann Glenn?" Before I could answer him there was another one pushing me off the fence, while a third one was throwing me in cuffs. Within 45 minutes I was being processed at Loudoun County ADC. I figured they would give me low bond, or release me on my own recognizance. I was wrong. Needless to say I had an interesting summer vacation.

"and the rain descended, the floods came" I was charged with malicious wounding, a crime with stiff consequences if you're not aware. I spent my 21st birthday in that jail, and never was a conversation with my Mother more meaningful. I had a Bible, and I prayed. I was offered a deal reducing the malicious wounding to an unlawful wounding. I was told it would be a deferred finding, and after 2 years of probation my felony would be changed to a misdemeanor. Yet on my court date things played out very differently. The deal was changed to 5 years of probation, along with the felony conviction. What a difference 3 years can make, huh? From a promising future with the world at my feet, to a 21 year old convicted felon. Looking back, I realize I was in a deep depression and having a crisis with my self identity. I wasn't sure if I was still an intelligent young man with a future, or a convicted felon destined for a life of crime. Instead of digging in to the problem, all I did was neglect it. Which is always a first ingredient to making things worse.

I gave up on school, and returned home. My parents would constantly tell me I needed to get my education, but I had convinced myself there was a different kind of education for me. I was going to make it either rhyming or hustling. As time passed I found myself with a constant longing and emptiness inside that couldn't be filled with money, women, or drugs. I saw all the people I graduated high school with living their lives. Some were married, working in affluent careers, owning their own businesses......living that "American Dream." Then I looked at me, and what my life had turned in to. The stress of worrying was the package moving right. "Are these workers going to bring the money back right? Is somebody plotting on me? Have the police or federal agents caught on to me yet?" I had one very good friend from childhood who reached out to me by the name of Jason. Now "Robbe" (as we call him) would always be on me about getting a job. He would tell me about these women he was meeting, and he looked so carefree. So I decided to give it a try. I ended up excelling at the job, and decided I was going to leave the streets alone for good. That job proved to be a wonderful stepping stone in to my next position. At the next job I also excelled, and the compensation was INCREDIBLE!! In no time I was living the "corporate" lifestyle going to happy hour. I didn't have to lie to women about where my money was coming from any longer.

  At this point I feel it's necessary I tell you my view of women up to that point. I was never a disrespectful, "woman hating" type. Nope.....I was far worse. I was the type of guy who would tell a woman whatever she needed to hear, and then I would bounce once I was "satisfied." Needless to say, falling in love and marriage were never in the plans for me. I have loved and cared deeply for many women, yet I had never truly been "in love." My apologies to any women I may have hurt, I pray the Father has provided you with a mate who fulfills your needs and appreciates you for the wonderful person you are. Now let's flashback to the story.

While working one day a young lady came walking through the office on orientation. I was sitting next to my friend Brandon and before I could think about it I yelled out.....WHOOOO! She looked so good, and I was never one to hesitate, if you know what I mean. Eventually, she was hired and was in my department. For the first week or so I just stared at her from a distance. Truthfully for the first time in my life I was too intimidated to speak. At a cigarette break one day though, no one was outside but Brandon, her, and I. So I mustered a little courage and struck up a conversation. At some point I mentioned I was an emcee, so she told me to write her a rap. I got back to my desk and right to it! Never one to miss an opportunity, I ended the rap with my phone number. SHE NEVER CALLED. Yet, at work we did talk. Then finally one Saturday, she actually came by just to go get a bite to eat. We ended up spending the whole evening, until about 3 AM the next day, just talking. The conversation never turned to anything sexual, just conversed about life and God. Two days later we both admitted we liked each other but didn't want to seem to "thirsty". She came home with me after work, and Danielle became a HUGE part of my life. Remember though, I was still dealing with a lot of issues on the inside. I was paranoid from the life I had been living, I had never been a "boyfriend", and I wasn't used to somebody being "'all up in my business". There's another bit of advice I didn't pay heed to: it's not good to be in a relationship with someone you work with. We went through a lot of ups and downs, and because I had an anger problem I did what a man should never do. Yet, Danielle always saw my heart.....and God was in her. She would leave me for a season, but she was always there when I need her. Let me tell you guys, I messed up a **whole** lot.

Still God saw fit to continue blessing me. Danielle and I went through our changes, and we ended up living together. (For the record I am not condoning co-habitation.) I ended up losing my job, and returning back to the streets. *"....the floods came, and the winds blew and beat on that house...."* Danielle very quickly let me know she wasn't putting up with any of my mess. At the time I was drinking heavily, and had become quite abusive both physically and verbally towards her. The demons I had in me began to manifest themselves. One day I found myself with our home surrounded by officers, standing on the balcony holding a steak knife to my neck. Danielle and a very good friend named Amanda called the police because they could see I was "losing it". I was at a point that no matter where I looked, my life truly appeared hopeless. The police took me to Mt. Vernon where I stayed for three days in there psychiatric ward. I spoke with my Father who had admitted me, and against his good sense he agreed to let me be released. The day I was released a problem in the streets nearly took my life. That was the final straw for Danielle, within two weeks she was gone. I continued hustling, caught in a fantasy….refusing to admit my life was going the wrong way. I still had contact with Lady D, but there was definitely a distance. I had a good friend "Peanut" who stuck with me through this period. God placed him in my life, along with Jen, to help me get through this "rough patch." But me being me, I didn't listen…..I just kept doing whatever my desires directed.

In the midst of "doing me," I ended up with a possession of cocaine charge. *"and it fell."* Next thing I knew, I was all alone. I found myself homeless. I was sleeping in the dugout at the Herndon Community Center, and the laundry room in Elden Terrace. I didn't have enough money to get any more drugs to sell, so I was surviving by pure deception. I stumbled into the barbershop and the brothers there looked out for me. Right now I want to thank all of you; Erk, Big D (GO COWBOYS!), Millz, Will, AB DA BUTCHA, and all the customers. They gave me an opportunity to begin cutting hair, but I just wanted to get back to hustling. In time I started lying and robbing everybody I could. After burning almost every bridge in my life, I got "back up on my feet," with more enemies than I truly realized. I didn't take the charge I was facing seriously and eventually got arrested for skipping my court date. I plead guilty, and was released on my bond again. My parents let me move

Job 32:18

back in, but I still chose to be in the streets. I had a great friend named Tariq who looked out for me. I love him, his mother, and his father. they were truly there in my time of need. I couldn't see it, but God was all around me protecting me, if only I would have opened my eyes.

I was beaten pretty bad because I had conned someone out of their money, and my eyes were severely damaged. Not long after I was supposed to go back to court and be sentenced. That morning I got up, but I couldn't move my legs. My friend Jesse took me to the hospital they ran a few tests and said I probably had some clots. I was supposed to go back and get checked up, but I knew when I left there I wasn't ever going to do a follow up. Once again I missed my court date. I called my Mom to let her know, and she informed me my Father had a stroke and was in the same hospital. Immediately I went up to I.C.U. and sat with him for a few hours. The next day I moved back in to my parent's house. I got a job and began to do whatever they needed to help them out. The job lasted about two months, and then I was back in to "entrepreneurship." The evening before Thanksgiving 2008 I was pulled over and arrested because of the sentencing date I missed in July of that year. I was sentenced and released on probation in January of 2009 once again homeless.

Upon my release I called Danielle, just to let her know I was out and would love to get back in touch. A few days later she called back, and ironically she was going through a rough time herself. She picked me up and after we discussed our problems she allowed me to move in with her. A very close friend named Kathy helped me out with employment, and I was even contemplating getting some training in either culinary arts or electrician apprenticeship. God was putting my life together and, slowly but surely, was strengthening the bond between Danielle and I. Eventually I got comfortable and began taking life for granted. Instead of counting my blessings, I found myself wanting to get back out in those streets. Soon I was back to selling cocaine, drinking, and back on the track of self destruction. One evening I came in from work, at the time Danielle and I were having some hard times. A simple conversation turned into a HUGE blowout.

"and it fell. And great was its fall." I put my hands on Danielle, and physically abused her in a way I didn't think I was capable of. We went to the hospital, and not long after we arrived the police arrested me. Four days later I was in an isolation cell, with both of my hands broken, and nothing to read but "Our Daily Bread." On that fourth evening, June 16, 2009, I found myself curled up like an infant crying out to the Father for direction. I prayed like I had never prayed before, I had finally hit rock bottom. I looked around at my life and realized that I had destroyed myself and everyone else around me. I begged God to come in to my life and show me a better way. I couldn't take it any more; the weight of life had gotten to heavy. My parents needed me to be a good son and be there for them. My siblings needed me to be a good brother and live up to my potential. Danielle deserved more than what I was putting her through. I knew only God could mold me in to the man I should be.

Over the next two weeks I dissected the Bible like I had never before. Upon completion God opened a door for me to be bailed out, and I went to live with my parents. **"Therefore whoever hears these sayings of Mine and does them, I will liken him to a wise man who built his house on the rock"** While there I re-connected with my family, and began to care for my Father. I also began to attend church again; even went to Vacation Bible School. God began to renew the calling He placed on my life. Mrs. Parker was teaching a class on spiritual gifting, and though I didn't have the funds to attend God made a way. In hindsight, I see now He was preparing me and answering my prayer for Him to guide me. On September 21, 2009 my father passed away. Oddly I was at peace with it. I know now that God had me released so I could spend the last two months of my father's life with him....and I appreciated it. Still, I had to deal with my legal issues, and on October 14, 2009 I surrendered myself to Fairfax County on my probation violations.

"And the rain descended, the floods came, and the winds blew and beat on that house" My only concern when I turned myself in was strengthening my relationship with God, and answering the call on my life. Incarceration can be beneficial or detrimental based on a number of factors. The first unit I found myself in had another inmate by the name of J.D. who knew my father and brother. Which was a great relief, I'm not sure if he knows it.....but just knowing he knew my family provided immeasurable comfort. I couldn't get a Bible for about a month, so I indulged in conversations that did not edify my spirit. Yet I prayed every night, and for the first time in a long time I could hear the Father audibly. I began attending some Bible studies, and I met the chaplain. Chaplain Bob Milne was a God send! He mentored me, prayed with me, and was as concerned about my spiritual well-being as another human could be; strengthening my faith and resolve to continue following the Father. I began to conduct Bible studies and counsel brothers in the cell blocks I was assigned to. I learned meditation, and God revealed the plans for my future. This is the time He showed me C.H.O.I.C.E.S., Frontline Faith, as well as Mustard Seed Ministry. I also began to write Spirit inspired sermons. I was sentenced to two years in Fairfax County, and then transferred to Prince William County for sentencing on my crime against Danielle.

Prince William County offers a faith-based program known as the M.I.N.D. dorm, which provided me with much needed resources for continued growth in the Spirit. It also afforded me the opportunity to be around other brothers who were dedicated to God, and a chance to meet some wonderful speakers. Speakers who inspired me, and mentored me in ways they probably don't realize. I was sentenced to two years and eleven months in Prince William County. Instead of being down though, I just prayed the Father use me in anyway he needed me.

"and it did not fall, for it was founded on the rock." I write these words as I sit in the M.I.N.D. dorm here at Prince William County. I'm still maturing into whom God would have me be, and I am amazed at the ways He is using me. I am hopeful, and know that I am a better today than I've ever been. I have no concerns for my future, God has laid the path.....my only responsibility is to follow. Currently my release date is winter of 2013. I pray the Father use me between now and then to carry out His work. To inspire His people, whether free or incarcerated. My brothers and sisters, regardless of your physical circumstance.....place your faith in the Father. He will give you the ability and strength to make it through life's storms. From time to time in here I get a little down, but God will send someone to shed some sunshine. I don't listen when the enemy tries to invade my mind with thoughts of my former self, with doubts of self, or with urges to revert to old ways of thinking. I stand firm on the promises in the Word, **I know** I am redeemed.

 I pray you are encouraged by my testimony. I know someone out there is going through it right now, and I want to let you know you don't have to go it alone. None of us are sure what the future holds, but God is. Get on one accord with Him, don't waste time like I did.

Mustard Seed Ministries

BE BLESSED BE FAITHFUL

Job 32:18

OBEDIENCE

"He who has my commandments and keeps them, it is he who loves Me. And he who loves Me will be loved by my Father, and I will love him and manifest Myself to him."
(John 14:21 NKJV)

Through my study of scripture, I've recognized there some things the Father requires of us as believers. We must accept Christ as our Savior, live peacefully, be giving, honest, share our faith, and witness to others. The list goes on, and all of them don't seem very unreasonable. I have discovered they're all of equal importance. Yet, to me, one is a little harder than the others for most of us..... **obedience**. Adherence to this cause is key to success in all the rest. You can be as faithful, bold, peaceful and honest as you want to be. If these are not done out of obedience, rather than self glorification, it will have a negative effect on your testimony and relationship with Him. In today's key verse it reads, .<u>**"He who has my commandments and keeps them, it is he who loves Me."**</u> Emphasis on.....KEEPS THEM. Jesus doesn't say he who loves me, he who knows them, he who acknowledges them, or he who tells everyone what God has planned for them if they don't do His will. No.....it says <u>KEEPS THEM</u>. Simple. To the point, no need for deep analytical thought as to what is required.

What does this tell us about the importance of obedience? That it is a direct reflection of how much we love the Father. Now think about that for a second. Think about how obedient you've been in your life. Have you truly displayed how much you love the Father? I don't know about you, but I am thankful for grace and mercy. Because I know there is no possible way I've done that. How about you? Deeper than being a mere reflection of how much we love him: it

Job 32:18

is the only way to truly display the depth of our **recognition** and **appreciation** of His love for us. How often do we look at scriptures, read them, yet not grasp the magnitude of the words. Take a moment and read John 14:21 to yourself..... reflect on what it's **truly** saying. Reflect on 1 Kings 3:14 and see what he tells Solomon is the key to unlocking a long life.

I don't want to take up too much of your time, let's quickly look at a few examples of disobedience. We'll start with Saul. Now if you're not familiar with him, take some time out to read 1 Samuel. Here's a guy with no self-esteem, lowest man on the totem pole, from the smallest tribe amongst the Israelites, the least likely candidate to be King of the nation of Israel. Yet God takes him, and exalts him to this position. As with most people though, once on top he forget from whence he came. Soon Saul becomes disobedient, making decisions without God's consent, and against God's will. God doesn't waste any time wiping him and his entire lineage right off the map...save one crippled grandson.

Look at Jonah, three days in the belly of a whale, because he didn't want to listen. Thought he could run from God. How many of you know a man running from God is a dangerous man? See, when you're running from God, you're outside of his will, outside of his protection. Leaving you open to any and all attacks. Guess who's probably going to be attacking you now? Any guesses? Lucifer, Satan, the Evil One!!! Now you're being attacked by an enemy you can't possibly defeat, not armed with the necessary weapons to protect yourself. WHY? What is the catalyst of this catastrophe....you ask. (GASP!!) Because you're not being obedient.

All of our problems in life come from a lack of obedience. Children, find yourself on punishment...you weren't obedient to your parents. Husbands, find yourself fired from your job...you probably weren't obedient to your boss. Wives, find yourself being ignored by your husbands... good chance you're not being obedient to his needs. Health problems stem from not being obedient to proper diet and exercise. Car problems are usually rooted in not being obedient to proper maintenance. Get the picture. Here's the question. If obedience affects so many of the things in your carnal life, how on earth do you think it's not just as paramount in your spiritual life? Oh, that Benz goes to the dealership promptly every 3,000 miles. We count calories, and hit the gym fanatically. "I can't lose my job; I'm going to have to put in some overtime." "I love my man... let me make him something special, I know he's having a hard week." Oh, we're quick to be obedient to the things of this world. Let me ask you, when was the last time you were quick to be obedient to the word of God? When is the last time you went out of your way to help a stranger? When is the last time you called on his strength to restrain you from that "little 'ol sin" that everybody commits? When is the last time you sat down with your children and read to them from the Bible? When is the last time you put in some <u>overtime</u> studying the Word?

Job 32:18

See, all the pomp and ritual of Sunday morning means nothing, if you're not obedient on Saturday night when Ms. "Right Now" asks you to come upstairs. All the Hallelujah's don't mean much at the revival, if the night before you were cussing out your loved ones. Let me tell you a little secret, when judgment comes.....you won't be able to "blame it on the alcohol." Be obedient to the word, to the example Jesus left for you to follow. I would hate on the Day of Judgment for him to say he doesn't know you. It warns us many will say we do works in his names, and he will tell us just that. *Matthew 7:23 NKJV... "And then I will declare to them, I never knew you; depart from Me, you who practice lawlessness!"* Look at that last word....<u>lawlessness</u>. What law do you think Jesus is referring to? Here's a hint.....when the time comes He's speaking about .The Constitution of The United States won't matter anymore. Get your lives in order right now.

More importantly the last part of our subject scripture is*..." and I will love him and manifest Myself to him."* Don't you want to have that personal relationship with the Father? Don't you want him to speak to **you**, and make himself known to **you**? Don't you want to truly appreciate His **LOVE**? Let me tell you, there's nothing else like it. Nothing more we can search for, or ever hope to find. People become addicted to a variety of "things" searching for this love. Whenever you see someone with a longing and emptiness that can't be filled....it is usually because they've failed to recognize His love. I don't know why people lack this love in all cases. I guarantee a vast majority of those cases is because they chose to be disobedient to God's law in their lives. See, we can't properly discern his will without knowing his law and abiding in it. Amen?

Choose today to turn away from the ways of this world in your heart. Choose to follow His law and will, repent of the old you and put on the new man. Let your actions reflect this change. Because if you'll just be obedient, He will love and manifest himself to you. What more could you want, what more could you ask for?

BE BLESSED BE FAITHFUL

FORGIVENESS

"As far as the east is from the west, So far has He removed our transgressions from us. As a father pities his children, So the Lord pities those who fear Him." (Psalms 103:12-13 NKJV)

"For if you forgive men their trespasses, your heavenly father will also forgive you. But if you do not forgive men their trespasses, neither will your Father forgive your trespasses." (Matthew 6:14-15 NKJV)

"Therefore I say to you, her sins, which are many, are forgiven, for she loved much. But to whom little is forgiven, the same loves little." (Luke 7:47 NKJV)

"Wash yourselves, make yourselves clean; put away the evil of your doings from before My eyes. Cease to do evil, Learn to do good; Seek justice, Rebuke the oppressor; Defend the fatherless, Plead for the widow." (Isaiah 1:16 NKJV)

"If you forgive the sins of any, they are forgiven them; if you retain the sins of any, they are retained."
(John 20:23 NKJV)

Job 32:18

    <u>Forgiveness;</u> this is probably the single most discussed topic amongst Christians. It is awesome when we take a step back and understand the depth of the Father's forgiveness for us, isn't it? Imagine if it were you in His shoes. This person you love so deeply, continuously turns their back on you. You sacrifice your <u>only</u> begotten Son for them, and they still have the gall to curse you. Bail a person out of their problems time and time again, and rarely receive a thank you. Make your self available to fulfill all of a person's needs, yet you only hear from them when they find themselves in a bad situation. They never share their joys with you, only their pains. You offer them life, and they mockingly choose death.

    Looks different when you take that point of view doesn't it? Probably saying to yourself, "Y'all ought to be glad I'm not on the throne, because Hell would be overcrowded!" **AMEN**? Take a moment where ever you are right now, and offer your Father some thanks.....offer Him some praise.....show some appreciation right now.

    Very often though, people have a skewed view of the forgiveness concept. Most feel as though forgiveness is afforded once you're baptized, no matter what you do, He will forgive you. Well you've sort of got it right. Allow me to inform you that sort of isn't going to get you in those pearly gates though? So let's clear up some of the misconceptions right now. Turn to 1 John 1:9; here it reads, ***"If we confess our sins, He is faithful and just to forgive us our sins and to cleanse us from all unrighteousness."*** *(NKJV)* Did you see it? That little part that says *"If we"*, yup that's the part right there. That means we have to do something, in order to receive forgiveness. It isn't just attributed to you because you go to Church every Sunday, organize homeless drives, and do every other good deed under the sun. No, God wants us to take responsibility for our actions and ask Him to forgive us. Does that seem to hard? Not to me, probably not to you either.....yet many of us forget this crucial step in the forgiveness process. Don't get caught in your sin on the day of judgment because you didn't ask Him. Doesn't it just seem like we're taking advantage of His forgiving nature by assuming were forgiven? I was taught as a youngster the only way to receive something is to ask for it. Why would you think this concept does not also refer to things we need from God? He knows your needs, yet He does not act on them until you ask Him to. Free will people, free will..

    I assume we are all familiar with the adage, "you get what you give." This concept also applies to forgiveness. ***"For if you forgive men their trespasses, your heavenly Father will also forgive you. But if you do not forgive men their trespasses, neither will your Father forgive your trespasses.(Matthew 6:14-15 NKJV)*** Yes brothers and sisters, here we see another crucial element in God's forgiveness. This step is hard for many of us, because sometimes people just cross the line. I know I used to always say, "Once you cross certain lines....you have to deal with the consequences." But who was, and who am, I to condemn another person? That type of judgment is

Job 32:18

reserved for God and God alone. Where would we be if God treated us in this manner? We forgive others not to make ourselves or them feel better, but we forgive them because it is our duty. We forgive them out of appreciation for God's forgiveness of our wrongs. This duty also pertains to the authority afforded us as disciples' of Christ. **"If you forgive the sins of any, they are forgiven them; if you retain the sins of any, they are retained," (John 20:23 NKJV).** These are the words of Jesus for those of you who don't have your bible handy, those beautiful red letters. God knows that He has entrusted us with his Spirit, so He trusts our decisions when they are spiritually discerned. Yes, I was just saying to myself... *"This forgiveness thing sure carries a lot of responsibility."* These two passages vividly demonstrate the importance of our forgiveness of others in relationship to our own forgiveness from God. So next time you decide to hold a grudge ask yourself how would you feel if God held that grudge against you. The next time you find yourself not wanting to forgive someone ask yourself; "Is their offense so great that God in heaven wouldn't forgive them?" Put on the mind of Christ in all of your decisions, especially the ones that truly cause battles between your carnal and spiritual self. Our humanity will often require we make one decision, but God demands we make the other. Remember as believers we are not living for the here and now, but for the whole of eternity.

It should be no surprise that another HUGE factor in forgiveness is love. We all know that God is love. In fact I often interchange the two words when reading scripture. Try it sometime; you'd be amazed how the meaning of the passage doesn't change. Let us take a look at Luke 7:47(NKJ17), ***"Therefore I say to you, her sins, Which are many, are forgiven, for she loved much. But to whom little is forgiven, the same loves little."*** I don't know about you, but I have a lot I need to be forgiven of. In fact I almost guarantee by the time I'm finished writing this, I'll be in need of forgiveness for something that has entered my mind. How about you? See the more love (God) is in your heart, the more prone to forgive you are. Yet, if there is a lack of love (God) in your heart the less likely you will be to forgive. How can God forgive you, if you don't believe He will? How can you believe He will, unless you have Him in your heart and are able to recognize His presence? Forgiveness, true forgiveness can only come from God. Therefore you can only truly forgive another if you have God in you. If you have God in you, your actions will be like His. The same measure of forgiveness He has afforded to you, you will naturally offer to others. ***"And above all things have fervent love for one another, for "love will cover a multitude of sins."*** (1 Peter 4:8 NKJV) This passage in 1 Peter helps drive the need for love home doesn't it? I'm not the most intelligent soul,, but covering a multitude of sins sounds like forgiveness to me.

Another wonderful thing about the Father's forgiveness is it's forever and ever. He doesn't remember it anymore, once you come to Him and ask forgiveness. ***"As far as the east is from the west, So far has He removed our transgressions from us. As a father pities his children, so the Lord pities those who fear Him."*** (Psalms 103:12-13 NKIV) The first time I read this statement the passage "east from the west" made me think of the distance between L.A and New York. Yet when I took the time to dig in to it, the distance is more like the one between the Sun and Pluto. Think cardinal points, not any tangible point. That is an awesome type of forgiveness, wouldn't you agree? It makes sense though because we know that God **HATES** sin. He doesn't dislike it, it doesn't mildly annoy Him, He **HATES** it. Yet He loves us and wants us in His presence thus creating a dilemma. Of course Him being God, He's got a way to circumvent this dilemma. You guessed it.....by offering up Jesus and opening a door for eternal forgiveness. Look at the statement, ***"As a father pities his children, so the Lord pities those who fear Him."*** Yes, that is the way He feels about each of us who humble ourselves in His sight. The type of fear spoken of here is reverential. I've always viewed this as a divine respect. We show respect to the Father when we go to Him and ask for forgiveness. To do otherwise would be to think that we don't need or we don't care about His feelings toward sin. Either way that's not the type of attitude that we should take with Him. Let's take the attitude of the "troublesome children" we are, and our need to go to the Father. Remember when you were a kid and got caught doing something wrong, what made your parents so upset? The fact that you disobeyed them, they still loved you whether you asked for forgiveness or not, correct? That love they had for you is what inevitably made you want to seek their forgiveness. I ask you, if the love God has for you is greater than that your parents have for you, how much more compelled should you be to seek His forgiveness? If you haven't done it recently don't waste another minute, go to the Father now and ask forgiveness.

Once you have done this, then continue on doing the work He's sent you forth to do. ***"Wash yourselves, make yourselves clean; Put away the evil of your doings from before My eyes. Cease to do evil, Learn to do good; Seek justice, Rebuke the oppressor; Defend the fatherless, Plead for the widow."*** (Isaiah 1:16 NKJV) These words in Isaiah are instructions for all of us. Once we have experienced the forgiveness and mercy of our Father, we should not return to our sins. Our actions should reflect the love and forgiveness that has been bestowed upon us. I challenge each of you today to make the decision to do this in your lives; to go forth and allow your life to reflect the Father inside of you. In actuality, forgiveness all boils down to this: Ask for it and give it to others just like every other gift of the Father. Live for God, die to self. I'll be praying for you.

Job 32:18

BE BLESSED BE FAITHFUL

POWER OF WORDS

"Who is the man who desires life, And loves many days, that he may see good? Keep your tongue from evil, And your lips from deceit."
(Psalm 34:12-13 NKJV)

"For by your words you will be justified, and by your words you will be condemned."
(Matthew 12:37 NKJV)

"For we all stumble in many things. If anyone does not stumble in word, he is a perfect man, able to also bridle the whole body."
" But no man can tame the tongue. It is an unruly evil full of deadly poison."
(James 3:2, 8 NKJV)

"Not what goes in to the mouth defiles a man; but what comes out of the mouth; this defiles a man."
(Matthew 15:11 NKJV)

"Sticks and stones may break my bones, but words will never hurt me!" How many times have we heard others and ourselves say this little phrase. I bet if you had a dollar for every time you heard it, you'd be travelling the world uninhibited; with no care for the cost of food, clothing, travel, or housing. What a perfect world it would be if these little saying were true. "Sticks and stones may break my bones, but words will never hurt me!" Let's put this little saying to the test.

"I hate you!" "You're stupid!" "You'll never amount to anything!" "Why don't you just die?" "You are ugly and fat!" "Sticks and stones may break my bones but words will never hurt me?" Do you still think that little saying rings so true now? When is the last time you really analyzed the power of words, there ability to tear down and build up? The bible has many scriptures which address this truth, I've chosen but a few for us to look over today.

"In the beginning was the Word and the Word was with God, and the Word was God." (John 1:1 NKJV) For all of my Bible scholars, we know this passage describes Jesus Christ. Yet, look at what word is used to describe Him, **WORD.** The majesty, strength, power, hope, and fulfillment of prophecy that is Jesus all summed up in one word.....**WORD.** Let's look back at Genesis.... ***"Then God said, 'Let there be light'; And there was light."*** (Genesis 1:3 NKJV) It doesn't say He snapped His fingers, clapped His hands, thought, or anything else. It reads, ***"THEN GOD SAID."*** I'm not sure about you, but "said" usually means one has to have spoken. If one is speaking, it's fairly safe to they are using, you guessed it, <u>WORDS.</u> So in the 3rd verse, of the first chapter, of the first book, of the **Bible** we see God wielding the power of the **<u>WORD.</u>** Why do you think God himself puts such an emphasis on words? Wouldn't take an Ivy Leaguer to comprehend He's obviously trying to clue us in on the strength of what we speak.

Wars are started by them, wars are ended with them. Lives are saved by them, lives are taken with them. They are the primary form of communication between human beings. In fact it is not possible for anything in our lives to take place without them. ***"<u>Who is the man who desires life, And loves many days, that he may see good? Keep your tongue from evil, And your lips from deceit.</u>"*** (Psalm 34:12-13 NKJV) Here in scripture we are shown the direct correlation that life and death hinges on the words we use. The first part of the text poses a question, a question I would assume we would all. Answer, "yes" to. Then an answer is given on how a man may have, "life, and loves many days that he may see good..." Amazingly, it involves watching what one says. We know that we live in treacherous times, where many have no sense of life's true value. We see lives taken for far less than a word exchanged in haste, so we are fully aware that people die for a misplaced comment. Yes, it is sad, horrifying, and a direct contradiction of why God created us. Yet, it is a part of this life's compromised reality and one of the tribulations we must live with. Knowing the world is this way, we should be guarded in our words so our lives aren't ended in some senseless manner.

To take it a step further; whom we allow into our homes, or even carry on conversations with says a lot about us. These and many other aspects of our lives are initiated by invitation, and acceptance of others invitations. Watch use of that word everyone loves....."YES." It can open up a world of trouble we don't even see coming.

On a spiritual level, we know that God holds every word we say up to His divine code. On the Day of Judgment we will have to answer for our words, just as much as our actions. Jesus tells us this, ***"For by your words you will be justified, and by your words you will be condemned."*** (Matthew 12:37 NKJV) So yes, what man will do to you for speaking the wrong words is horrible, but what God will do for improper use of our words should be more of a concern. I feel like everyone else, I'd like to avoid as much physical pain as possible. Yet, the prospect of eternal spiritual death tends to be a bigger motivator for me. Jesus also said, ***"Therefore whoever confesses Me before men, him I will also confess before My Father who is in heaven. But whoever denies Me before men, him I will also deny before My Father who is in heaven."*** (Matthew 10:32-33) This tells us, not only will we be judged for what we do say, but also for what **we do not** say, The Lord requires an open, verbal confession of our belief in Him. It's not enough to just know it in your heart.

You have to let others know, not just through actions, but also through your words. Ask yourself, if today were that "great gittin' up mawning"....how would you rate in this category?

We're not perfect, and God knows it... how thankful all of us should be that God knows it. Knows it so much, he sent His only begotten Son to save our filthy, impure souls. ***"For we all stumble in many things. If anyone does not stumble in word, he is a perfect man, able to also bridle the whole body. "*** (James 3:2 NKJV) Don't get down on yourself because you're not perfect. Also, realizing you're not perfect doesn't give you a license to just continue doing the wrong thing. Just pray, ask God for strength to control the words you speak. I myself find it's more than just the words that come from my mouth, but even the thoughts in my mind. The same way we pray for everything else we want, let's begin to pray for what He wants for us. Let's begin to pray that the Holy Spirit perfect every aspect of us. Not just the parts we want. ***"But no man can tame the tongue. It is an unruly evil, full of deadly poison."*** (James 3:8 NKJV) Right here James tells us that we don't have the power to control our words. The only way to receive the power, is to draw on the Holy Spirit. So don't hesitate, make the choice today to do as such. When you go in to your prayer closet and you're praying for everything your heart desires; take the time to pray that God control your words, because they play a <u>huge</u> part in your spiritual <u>life</u> as well. ***"Set a guard, 0 Lord, over my mouth; Keep watch***

over the door of my lips. Do not incline my heart to any evil thing, To practice wicked works With men who work iniquity; And do not let me eat of their delicacies." (Psalms 141:3-4 NKJV)

Last but not least, we know the words we speak determine how others perceive us. 2 Corinthians 6:3 (NKJV) reads, ***"We give no offense in anything, that our ministry may not be blamed."*** As Christians, we know it is our purpose to spread God's Word to the world. We can't do that, if we act and speak improperly. Ask yourself, if you were the only person in the world who was a Christian, would you be an accurate description of what a Christian is? Hmmmm. If not, then you must take a self inventory and begin to walk upright as the Lord would have you to. You may be the only Christian a person ever meets. You may be the only opportunity a person gets to be exposed to the one and only way to eternal life. Heaven forbid they miss the message because of the messenger. Ask yourself, "In my life, have there been people who may have gotten the wrong impression of Christianity because of my "word selection" day to day?" If they see you cursing, making lewd comments, gossiping, etc.... do you think that seems very appealing? Is it an accurate portrayal of what God requires of His believers?

"Not what goes into the mouth defiles a man; but what comes out of the mouth, this defiles a man." (Matthew 15:11 NKJV) Remember this scripture in your daily life. Jesus spoke these words, when questioned about the disciples not washing their hands before eating food. If you didn't know, the Jewish law required one to wash their hands before eating. Great law, it's good and sanitary. I'm sure even in your own household you follow this rule. I'm sure Jesus didn't have a problem with sanitary living, yet understand Jesus' point here. It means <u>nothing</u> if your body is clean and the food you eat is clean, that only affects you. Our lives are meant to be living sacrifices to the Lord. Our actions are meant to be reflections of our Heavenly Father. A tree is judged by the fruit it bears, a tree of God should bear Godly fruit and benefits. What comes out of us is very important in furthering the Gospel, because people's perception of us affects how they receive our witness. I think instead of saying, "Sticks and stones may break my bones, but words will never hurt me." We should say, "Sticks and stones may break my bones, but words affect us eternally." Choose your words carefully…Very carefully.

BE BLESSED BE FAITHFUL

Job 32:18

POWER OF THOUGHTS

"Blessed is the man Who walks not in the counsel of the ungodly, Nor stands in the path of sinners, Nor sits in the seat of the scornful; But his delight is in the law of the Lord, And in His law he meditates day and night."
(Psalms 1:1-2 NKJV)

"Finally, brethren, whatever things are true, whatever things are noble, whatever things are just, whatever things are pure, whatever things are lovely, whatever things are of good report, if there is any virtue and if there is anything praiseworthy –meditate on these things."
(Philippians 4:8 NKJV)

"Set your mind on things above, not on things on the earth"
(Colossians 3:2 NKJV)

How many of you know that what's on your mind, is usually what you end up doing? If you sit around all day thinking you're depressed, nine out of ten times you'll be depressed. If you go into a situation feeling like a winner, you'll probably win, Our state of mind, and thoughts determine more about our lives than people really pay heed to. I have spoken previously on the power of the words we use, I want to take it a step further and talk about our thoughts. In the battlefield of our mind many battles are waged and lost. As we all reflect on our lives we will be able to identify times when our thoughts were more detrimental than any other force on earth.

"Blessed is the man Who walks not in the counsel of the ungodly, Nor stands in the path of sinners, Nor sits in the seat of the scornful; But his delight is in the law of the Lord, And in His law he meditates day and night." (Psalms 1:1-2 NKJV) This passage touches on another subject we will address as well, the company we keep. If we find ourselves bombarded by thoughts which are not from the Father, look no further than the people around you to find the root of them. If we partake of conversations and activities that are ungodly, our thoughts will begin to reflect ungodliness as well. Our self-image is largely based on those we associate with, and the activities we participate in. Therefore, surround yourself with God and godly people. Naturally the actions you take will be God centered, rather than flesh centered. That is why David describes a blessed man as one who's ***"delight is in the law of the Lord,***

Job 32:18

And in His law he meditates day and night." Nothing in the Father's word will cause you to be depressed, or commit acts of self-destruction. On the contrary, the Word will inspire you to be more God like. Your **thoughts** of self and life in general will be elevated. Instead of looking at the surface, you will begin to delve deeper and unlock the hidden mysteries of life. With your thoughts changed, your actions will naturally follow. If you fill your mind with blessed thoughts, you will have blessed actions. Those blessed actions will bless others and inevitably bless you.

Don't sit around thinking about how to get the nicest car, because once attained then what will happen? Rather spend your time thinking about the things which are eternal. Fill your mind with eternity, and you will take actions which have eternal effect. Fill your mind with the temporary, and you will only do things that fulfill you temporarily. This train of thought includes raising children, the work we do, the way we interact with others, even self grooming. Stop taking a temporary viewpoint on life, take an eternal viewpoint.....and watch the revelations you begin to have in your life.

For a lot of us the problem is recognizing what things are actually good, and what are bad. The first thing one must do is to view all things from a spiritual perspective. As humans, we can rationalize everything as being right. Yet, a lot of what we perceive to be right we know is contrary to God's view. Sex outside of marriage feels wonderful, yet in God's sight it is a serious no-no. Get the picture? Philippians 4:8 NKJV states, ***"Finally, brethren, whatever things are true, whatever things are noble, whatever things are just, whatever things are pure, whatever things are lovely, whatever things are of good report, if there is any virtue and if there is anything praiseworthy - meditate on these things."*** Don't you just love God? He lays it out, and it's always easy to grasp isn't it? Highlight this verse in your Bible, read it to your children, give it to your brothers and sisters when you see them feeling down. First it tells you *"whatever things are true, whatever things are noble, whatever things are just, whatever things are pure"*; doesn't matter if you've got a Doctorate or dropped out of school.....we can all recognize these things in life. It goes on to say, *"whatever things are lovely, whatever things are of good report"*; see there my brothers its o.k. to admire a beautiful woman. Yet be mindful that your thoughts are of "good report". AMEN? Finally it ends saying, *"if there is any virtue and if there is anything praiseworthy - meditate on these things."* Simply put if the thought in question has spiritual value and is pleasing to God, meditate on it. I often call this the **"Roadmap to the Land of Righteous Thought"**

     I can't stress enough the need to control your thoughts brothers and sisters. As I said before in the battlefield of your mind, many battles are won and lost. Often in my prayers I pray that God protect my mind, because I realize that Satan attacks there most often and violently. Usually it begins by justifying "small things" that I know are outside of God's will. Before long I find myself justifying any and everything my little heart desires. Remember, **_"For God is not the author of confusion but of peace, as in all the churches of the saints."_** (1 Corinthians 14:33 NKJV) If you sense yourself wondering if something is right or wrong, most times it's wrong. Don't listen to that "little voice" who tells you; "The Bible doesn't speak specifically against this or that." My beloved that is the enemy, and it is one of his oldest tactics. Protect your mind, protect your heart. AMEN?_When all else fails remember God is simple and nothing is meant to confuse you. Anything in your life that seems complex isn't of God. I'm not saying there will not be challenges, what would life be without challenges? I am stating that God will <u>never</u> approach you with a task to accomplish without giving you the necessary tools and resources to achieve it. Put on the mind of Jesus in all you do, be at one with God. I often meditate on John 10:30 (NKJV) **_"I and My father are one."_** I know that in order for this statement to be true, all of my ways must be a reflection of the Father's. I'm going to leave you all with a memory/meditation verse. **_"Set your mind on things above, not on things on the earth."_** (Colossians 3:2 NKJV)

BE BLESSED BE FAITHFUL

POWER OF PRAYER (PART ONE)

"If I regard iniquity in my heart, The Lord will not hear. But certainly God has heard me; He has attended to the voice of my prayer. Blessed be God, who has not turned away my prayer, nor his mercy from me!"
(Psalms 66:18-20 NKJV)

"You lust and do not have. You murder and covet and cannot obtain. You fight and war. Yet you do not have because you do not ask. You ask and do not receive, because you ask amiss, that you may spend it on your pleasures."
(James 4:2-3 NKJV)

"Ask, and it will be given to you; seek, and you will find; knock, and it will be opened to you." (Matthew 7:7 NKJV)

"And whatever things you ask in prayer, believing, you will receive."
(Matthew 21:22 NKJV)

Job 32:18

As a child I remember being told, "Tell God whatever you want, and He'll give it to you every time." Oh, I used to hop on my little knees and pour my heart out. I mean every little thing I could think of I would send it right up in prayer. Not long after though I began to feel as though God must not be listening, or my elders were lying to me. Yet I pressed on, decided that maybe if I talked with better vocabulary it would be more pleasing to God. Then one day a Sunday school teacher began to explain prayer a little more in depth, and things became more clear. A lot of Christians today feel as though God isn't listening, or that someone has lied to them. Well I'm here to let you know, you're wrong on both accords.

God is not Santa Claus; he doesn't fill our every heart's desire. Why? Ask yourself how many of your hearts desires He would want associated with Him. Could you imagine going around telling people God gave or assisted you in some of your desires? Wow! I'll let you think on that one yourself, and move on. The first thing we must do is come to God with a pure, clean heart. We can not come to the Father with any sin or ill will in our heart. Remember...sin separates us from God. ***"If I regard iniquity in my heart, The Lord will not hear. But certainly God has heard me; He has attended to the voice of my prayer. Blessed be God, Who has not turned away my prayer, Nor his mercy from me!"*** (Psalms 66:18-20 NKJV) So anything sinful within hinders our ability to pray effectively because

He can't draw near enough to hear us. So before you go rattling off your "to do list" for God, make sure you do some self examination. Come before Him humbly, asking forgiveness for your wrongdoings, Go to your earthly brothers and make amends, 1 John 4:20(NKJV) reads, ***"If someone says, 'I love God,' and hates his brother, he is a liar; for he who does not love his brother whom he has seen, how can he love God whom he has not seen?"*** I suppose it goes with out saying that if you don't love God, He won't be doing much for you. AMEN? So be sure to come with a pure heart, in all ways. Remember He is God, He judges the inner thoughts. You may get past other people with a smile, but it doesn't work with Him.

    Secondly, we must be sure that our will is aligned with the Father's. He won't grant any and everything. Because as Christians our lives should be lived in submission to His, our prayers should reflect that. Our prayers should be for things that further His will being done here on earth. ***"You lust and do not have. You murder and covet and cannot obtain. You fight and war. Yet you do not have because you do not ask. You ask and do not receive, because you ask amiss, that you may spend it on your pleasures."*** (James 4:2-3 NKJV) Yes, I understand we should pray for ourselves, I see no issue with that. I do feel that the majority of our prayers should be for others. We know that being a Christian is about being a servant, and taking on an attitude of humility. Notice the above text says, "Yet you do not have because you

Job 32:18

do not <u>ask</u>." How often in your life have you not taken yours and others needs to God in prayer? We go to the bank and ask for a loan, we go to our significant others and plead forgiveness, we go to others and ask for acceptance, we even go work certain jobs for a sense of validation. All "things" and "needs" should be taken to the Father first. He will provide.

The second part of this text reads, "You ask and do not receive, because you ask amiss, that you may spend it on your pleasures." That goes back to what are your intentions when you go to the Father with your petitions. If you're asking for anything that glorifies you and not Him, you need to rethink your prayer. As I said before, as a Christian you are called to a life of service, not self indulgence.

Let's look at some of my favorite examples of answered prayer. We'll begin with King Hezekiah, turn to 2 Kings 20:3. Here we see King Hezekiah has just gotten the news he is fatally ill. Upon reading prior text, you will discover that Hezekiah was a righteous man, in fact it states in 2Kings 18:3; ***"And he did what was right in the sight of the Lord, according to all that his father David had done."*** Yet here just two chapters later we see that he is stricken with a fatal illness. ***"Remember now, O Lord, I pray, how I have walked before You in truth and with a loyal heart, and have done what was good in Your sight.' And Hezekiah wept bitterly."*** (2 Kings 20:3) This is a short prayer, but very powerful all the same. Notice <u>all</u> he asks of the Father is to remember his faithfulness. He doesn't ask the Lord for anything, he already knows the Lord will provide for Him. God answers him back in 2Kings 20:5-6; ***"Return and tell Hezekiah the leader of My people, 'Thus says the Lord, the God of David your father: "I have heard your prayer, I have seen your tears; surely I will heal you. On the third day you shall go up to the house of the Lord. And I will add to your days fifteen years. I will deliver you and this city from the hand of the king of Assyria; and I will defend this city for My own sake, and for the sake of my servant David."*** Short, powerful prayer with a majestic, powerful answer. Awesome God, huh?

Notice Hezekiah didn't use any flattering, flowing words....he simply came to the Lord humbly. Didn't ask for anything in particular, and look what the Lord gave him in return for the life he presented to the Father. Oh, I hope my life is as acceptable to the Father. I pray my faith may grow to the strength of Hezekiah's. If you read further in the Bible, you will see God even went so far as to give Hezekiah a sign. A short and humble prayer, offered by one living a life in obedience and faith to the Father. Actions truly speak louder than words, don't they? Amazing what praying with a pure heart can do?

Next, let's take a look at Elisha. For those who don't know, Elisha was the prophet who was mentored by Elijah. Elijah wasn't just any prophet, for he lived such a life before the Lord he didn't die a physical death. No, we see here in the 2nd chapter of Kings that he was swept up to heaven in a chariot of fire. Let's look at verse 9 though. ***"And so it was, when***

Job 32:18

they had crossed over, that Elijah said to Elisha, 'Ask! What may I do for you, before I am taken away from you?' Elisha said, 'Please let a double portion of your spirit be upon me." Now, this could be looked at as a request from student to teacher. Yet remember that all gifts and good things come from God. So inevitably Elisha, is asking God to pour out this blessing on him. Reading further we see there is a requirement that Elisha must be there when Elijah ascends, and he must pick up Elijah's mantle. Here *we* see that he must keep the faith, and be obedient to receive the blessing he's asked for. Elisha does these things, and let me just suggest you read 2Kings to see what he accomplished for the Lord. Once again, this is what a pure heart, obedience, and faith can produce when combined with prayer.

The last example of answered prayer I'll speak on today is Solomon. Yes, great King Solomon. In 1 Kings 3 we witness God offering Solomon whatever his heart desires. I mean, what if the Master of the Universe told you to ask for whatever you want and you can have it. Would you ask to be President, a doctor, cure for A.I.D.S., money....what would you ask for? I myself would have to spend the rest of this life praying for forgiveness if I even contemplated such a scenario. AMEN? Let's take a look at what Solomon asked for though. *"Therefore give to Your servant an understanding heart to judge Your people, that I may discern between good and evil. For who is able to judge this great people of yours."* (1 Kings 3:9 NKJV) Wow! Big difference from what most of us would have asked for, huh? He didn't ask for riches, women, or anything material. He simply asked God to give him the tools to lead His people properly. How humble, how pure, how obedient, how faithful? In case you're not aware, Solomon's prayer was granted.....a million fold. Not only did God give him what he asked for, he also blessed him with all the riches of the world. Lesson to be learned....God knows what you want, He wants to see if your going to put Him before you or not. A humble prayer to be a good servant to others, results in becoming the richest man to ever grace the face of the earth.

We see a man have 15 years added to his life, another given power to work God's miracles here on earth, and another given all the riches of the earth. In all these cases there is one common bond.....proper prayer. God wants to give you your heart's desire, He just requires you come to Him correctly. Would you take someone out on a date without showering, brushing your teeth, and putting on a clean outfit? Of course not, so why would you approach God with anything less than your best. ***"Delight yourself also in the Lord, and He shall give you the desires of your heart."*** (Psalms 37:4 NKJV) All you have to do is ask, hint: ***"Ask, and it will be given to you; seek, and you will find; knock, and it will be opened to you."*** (Matthew 7:7 NKJV) Why waste time and your breath asking anyone but the source of all to supply your needs? Go to the Father, properly, and lay it all out before Him. He's waiting for you, He's reaching out for you.

"And whatever things you ask in prayer, believing, you will receive." (Matthew 21:22 NKJV) This is one of the most important parts, as far as I'm concerned. You can get on your knees and pray for the rest of your life. If you don't have any faith that God is going to answer your prayers, it's a waste of time. In addition to coming to him humbly, with a pure heart, we must come to him with all our heart. That means in complete faith and belief of his ability to provide for us. ***"But let him ask in faith, with no doubting, for he who doubts is like a wave of the sea driven and tossed by the wind. For let not that man suppose that he will receive anything from the Lord; he is a double-minded man, unstable in all his ways."*** (James 1:6-8 NKJV) Nobody ever said it better than James.

BE BLESSED BE FAITHFUL

LEAD A HORSE TO WATER

"The coming of the lawless one is according to the working of Satan, with all power, signs, and lying wonders, and with all unrighteous deception among those who perish, because they did not receive the love of the truth, that they might be saved And for this reason God will send them strong delusion, that they should believe the lie, that they all may be condemned who did not believe the truth but had pleasure in unrighteousness."
(2 Thessalonians 2:9-12 NKJV)

"then the Lord knows how to deliver the godly out of temptations and reserve the unjust under punishment for the day judgment,"
(2 Peter 2:9 NKJV)

"But when they opposed him and blasphemed, he shook his garments and said to them, Your blood be upon your own

heads; I am clean. From now on I will go to the Gentiles."
(Acts 18:6 NKJV)

"Son of man, I have made you a watchman for the house of Israel; therefore hear a word from my mouth, and give them warning from Me: When I say to the wicked, 'You shall surely die,' and you give him no warning nor speak to warn the wicked from his wicked way, to save his life, that same wicked man shall die in his iniquity; but his blood I will require at your hand. Yet if you warn the wicked, and he does not turn from his wickedness, nor from his wicked way, he shall die in his iniquity; but you have delivered your soul"
(Ezekiel 3:17-19 NKJV)

"So then neither he who plants is anything, nor he who waters, but God who gives the increase." (1 Corinthians 3:7 NKJV)

This message is intended to encourage the "frustrated witness." We have all at one time or another found ourselves in this category. One person we truly care about just won't come around to accepting the truth that is the Gospel. No matter how many times they see the miraculous works God has performed in your life. We try every approach known to man; empathy, quoting scriptures, playing gospel music, inviting them to church outings, etc. Yet for some reason or another, they will not accept the salvation God has offered all of mankind. I myself used to have many sleepless nights. Constantly asking God to give me the right words to speak, the right approach to use. Then one day it dawned on me, it's not my job to make people accept the Gospel. Who am I to think I can change someone else's heart, only God can do that. Let's stop frustrating ourselves, and allow God to do His work. ***"So then neither he who plants is anything, nor he who waters, but God who gives the increase."*** (1 Corinthians 3:7 NKJV) This passage perfectly illustrates our dilemma. Here Paul tells us that the work we do is not as significant as we think it is, for it is actually God who does the work. He works <u>through</u> us to plant and water, but he decides when a person will blossom. Therefore do not concern yourself with "seeing" the harvest of your work, rather perform the work because He has sent you to do so.

God has sent you out as a disciple of His Gospel. Not as a tyrant to force people to accept it. From time to time we all get frustrated and feel as though we are wasting our breath. We tell people countless times about God's grace and mercy, and we also tell them of the consequences of disobedience to the Father. My brothers and sisters, that is all we can do. Let's look at Ezekiel, and see what God himself has to say about it. *"Son of man, I have made you a watchman for the house of Israel; therefore hear a word from my mouth, and give them warning from Me: When I say to the wicked, 'You shall surely die,' and you give him no warning, nor speak to warn the wicked from his wicked way, to save his life, that same wicked man shall die in his iniquity; but his blood I will require at your hand. Yet if you warn the wicked, and he does not turn from his wickedness, nor from his wicked way, he shall die in his iniquity; but you have delivered your soul."* This scripture begins with God's instructions for his followers. *"Son of man, I have made you a watchman for the house of Israel; therefore hear a word from my mouth, and give them warning from Me:"* As disciples of Christ this is our duty. We have been told the Gospel from the mouth of God Himself, Jesus Christ, and it is our duty to pass on these warnings and declarations to the rest of mankind. *" When I say to the wicked, 'You shall surely die,' and you give him no warning, nor speak to warn the wicked from his wicked way, to save his life, that same wicked man shall die in his iniquity; but his blood I will require at your hand."* We as His children know what our Father finds acceptable, and what will cause His wrath to come down upon mankind. This particular piece of the passage tells us that if we don't deliver the message we are responsible for their demise. God will not hold the unbelievers accountable, if we the believers didn't do our part to warn them. On the contrary, we will be held accountable. ***"Yet if you warned the wicked, and he does not turn from his wickedness, nor from his wicked way, he shall die in his iniquity; but you have delivered your soul."*** But see here what He tells us? You have no reason to beat yourself up if you've done what is required of you. If you have witnessed to the non-believer God's message, you are no longer responsible for the outcome of their decision. This is a sad reality for the vast majority of us, because we think of our loved ones; the people we are intimately attached to, and it is hard to accept the fact some of them will not accept salvation. Yet I challenge you to look at it from this perspective. While you sit and become depressed about these people, what about the others you're supposed to be witnessing to? Remember, once you give your life to the Lord, you no longer live for self your life is His now. ***"If anyone comes to Me and does not hate his father and mother, wife and children, brothers and sisters, yes, and his own life also, he cannot be My disciple." (Luke 14:26 NKJV)*** Keep this verse in mind my brothers and sisters. Of course God wants us to love our families, but nothing is to come before Him ……and His purpose.

Another reality we must deal with is all people are not going to accept the truth of Jesus Christ. Some people are so caught up in their lives they don't ever take the time to recognize who's truly in control. In 2 Thessalonians God warns us of these types, and what He will do in these situations. *"The coming of the lawless one is according to the works of Satan, with all power, signs, and lying wonders, and with all unrighteous deception among those who perish, because they did not receive the love of the truth, that they might be saved. And for this reason God will send them strong delusion, that they should believe the lie, that they all may be condemned who did not believe the truth but had pleasure in unrighteousness."* (2 Thessalonians 2;9-12 NKJV) See my brothers and sisters God is the one in control. It's not a matter of if you have witnessed to another properly, or if you've done something wrong. Some are just so mixed up in the world that they choose not to *" receive the love of the truth."* We all have family and friends like this. Some of them make this choice because of pasts hurts, because they have chosen other "things" to be their God, or because they have exalted "self" to a places only God should be. For whatever reason they choose to take that path, it goes on to say.....*" And for this reason God will send them strong delusion, that they should believe the lie, that they all may be condemned who did not believe the truth but had pleasure in unrighteousness."* I don't know about you, but the first time I read this text I couldn't understand it. How could God allow this to happen? It almost seems as though He encourages it. But you have to look at the key word in the whole text...." ***because they did not receive the love of the truth, that they might be saved."*** This is not a decision God made, but these people have chosen to make. We understand the concept of "free will," and this is one of the consequences of using it wrongly. Continue to spread the word, yet keep this in mind when you feel as though there is no fruit from your work. Make sure you are going where the Spirit leads you, very rarely will it lead you to a "field" that is not prepared to receive "seed."

    I often pray to the Father that I may speak boldly. That I may deliver His message as the Spirit puts it in my heart, so anyone offended with the following can take their offense to Him. Brothers and sisters, there are many sitting in the pew with you right now who are not truly accepting the Gospel. AMEN? Oh, there's probably somebody you have seen performing acts outside of God's will and they just blow you off. No matter how many times you try to tell them how God feels about sex outside of marriage, cohabitating, adultery, greed, being judgmental, and anything else you can imagine they ignore you. Some of them even go so far as to say nasty things about you behind your back, and make you seem like everything but a child of God. That's been happening since the church began; ***"But when they opposed him and blasphemed, he shook his garments and said to them, 'Your blood be upon your own heads; I am clean. From now on I will go to the Gentiles."*** (Acts 18:6 NKJV) And that is what we have to do as well. Just because they're sitting in church, on the Diaconate, teach in the Sunday school, tithe regularly....that does not mean they are right with God. You do your part for the Kingdom, and you make them aware of their offense towards the Father. You do it biblically, in a manner to edify them. It is their **choice** to heed the warning. From then on you wash your hands of the situation, pray for them, then go and spread the Word where the Spirit leads you.

Some of us may have to leave the churches we are members of, others may have to escort some people out of the congregation. There is no room for hypocritical, lukewarm, citizens in the Kingdom. Understand loved ones that many a lost soul is hindered from surrendering to Christ because of these hypocrites. These hypocrites look down their noses and judge these lost souls causing them to feel ostracized and unwelcomed in the Father's house. This is wrong! As Christ said, *"**When Jesus heard that, He said to them, 'Those who are well have no need of a physician, but those who are sick, But go and learn what this means: 'I desire mercy and not sacrifice.' For I did not come to call the righteous, but sinners, to repentance."*** (Matthew 9:12 NKJV) As I said earlier, be sure that you are spreading seed where the Spirit is leading you. If you plant in unfertile ground, how do you expect to reap a harvest?

Lastly my brothers and sisters, God will not forsake His people. There are numerous scriptures which point out this promise of the Father. Though it may seem as though one *is* not truly heeding the advice you're offering them, God knows their heart. He knows what His chosen ones are going through and He will not allow them to fall. ***"then the Lord knows how to deliver the godly out of temptations and reserve the unjust under punishment for the day of judgment,"*** (2Peter 2:9 NKJV) Yes my brothers and sisters, trust in God. At times we get so wrapped up in what we're doing, we forget the basic promises of the Father. Didn't He remember you, how long did it take before you came to the light? Secondly who knows us better than the Father? When the time is right, He knows exactly what to do to gather His flock. No longer spend time beating yourself up. Reference these verses, pray, and trust in the Father. Then meditate on this verse, ***"Therefore, my beloved brethren, be steadfast, immovable, always abounding in the work of the Lord knowing that your labor is not in vain in the Lord."*** (1 Corinthians 15:58 NKJV) Continue in your good works my beloved, do not let the enemy have the victory. Remove all doubts, fears, and anything else that may compromise your ability to spread this wonderful gift we've received from the Father.

BE BLESSED BE FAITHFUL

WE CAN LEARN FROM ANYONE

"But God has chosen the foolish things of this world to put to shame the wise, and God has chosen the weak things of the world to put to shame the mighty"
(1 Corinthians 1:27 NKJV)

"Let no one deceive himself. If anyone among you seems to be wise in this age, let him become a fool that he may become wise. For the wisdom of this world is foolishness with God. For it is written, 'He catches the wise in their own craftiness; and again,' The Lord knows the thoughts of the wise, that they are futile."
(1 Corinthians 3:18-20 NKJV)

"And if anyone thinks that he knows anything, he knows nothing yet as he ought to know."
(1 Corinthians 8:2 NKJV)

I remember my father often telling my brother, sisters, and I how much he learned from us. He would often tell us this when he saw us getting a little "full of ourselves." It was always something like, *"I learn something from you guys everyday, so you know you can learn from anyone. When we think we know it all is exactly when we show we know nothing at all."* Another of his favorite sayings was, *"The one thing a wise man knows is that he knows nothing at all,"* As I reflect on those conversations, I am ever so grateful to my father for teaching me these lessons. In my life I've been surprised with instruction from people and sources I would never imagine. Often times in life God will speak to us in unexpected ways to humble us, and show His power. God is not limited to your beliefs and. expectations of people. By limiting our expectations of others we miss out on many valuable lessons. Through my reading of the Bible I've come to find that most of God's most important messages came through unlikely vessels.

"But God has chosen the foolish things of this world to put to shame the wise, and God has chosen the weak thinks of the world to put to shame the mighty;" (1 Corinthians 1:27 NKJV) Our first text today from Paul sheds a light on God's ability to teach us. For God to show His majesty, He doesn't need the smartest or strongest people to carry out His missions. It must have seemed utterly foolish to those early disciples that God chose to use Paul. I'm sure Peter said to someone, "What is on God's mind? Why would people believe this man who persecutes us?"

Job 32:18

Didn't make any sense then, but looking back on it...who would've been a better choice than Paul?

Let's look back a little further though. Turn with me to Numbers 22. Here we learn of the "prophet" Balaam. God has consulted him and given him instructions to follow. Yet like most of us, Balaam has decided to follow the instructions the way he saw fit. In verse 21 we see Balaam on the road, headed to meet with Balak, against the instructions of God. Three times Balaam's donkey tries to save him from death. Balaam does what most of us would do in this situation, he begins to beat and curse the donkey. However, the "foolish" donkey is aware of the angel God has placed on the road to kill Balaam. In verse 30 we see the amazing power of God to use whatever He chooses to teach us a lesson. ***"So the donkey said to Balaam, 'Am I not your donkey on which you have ridden, ever since I became yours, to this day? Was I ever disposed to do this to you?' And he said, 'No.' Then the Lord opened Balaam's eyes, and he saw the Angel of the Lord standing in the way with His drawn sword in His hand; and he bowed his head and fell flat on his face."*** (Numbers 22:30-31 NKJV) That's right people God used a donkey....not a child, or a foolish man.....but a donkey! Makes you look back on your life and wonder how many times God spoke through an unlikely channel to deliver a message to you. Huh? Me too.

On the contrary, how many times have you been led astray by one you thought was wise? How many times have you heeded advice from the wrong source? As humans we often judge "books" by their covers, rather than at least skimming through a few chapters. Some of the best advice I've ever received was from unlikely sources. During my incarceration I have been blessed to be around a number of good brothers. Outside of the jail the same person may be an addict, thief, or just an outright deviant. Yet inside the walls, without life's stresses and temptations, their true self is often revealed. Some of the most practical advice I've ever heard came from many of these men. Advice on everything from raising children, the need for education, the pros and cons of U.S. government policy, and spirituality. ***"Let no one deceive himself. If anyone among you seems to be wise in this age, let him become a fool that he may become wise. For the wisdom of this world is foolishness with God. For it is written, 'He catches the wise in their own craftiness'; and again, 'The Lord knows the thoughts of the wise, that they may be futile."*** (1Corinthians 3:18-20 NKJV) This passage is one I often refer to when mediating between two groups with differing opinions. My purpose is to demonstrate how only God is truly correct, and in all situations we need to defer to the Bible, prayer, meditation and fasting to receive proper direction. Most times we get so caught up in our own beliefs and ideologies, we never take the time out to let God have His way.

"For the wisdom of the world is foolishness with God." I meditate on this particular piece of the text to remain humble. Whenever I may begin to feel as though I have attained a certain level of wisdom

Job 32:18

and understanding, I remind myself that His level will always be higher than mine. I can't possibly sit around and question Him, nor try to think for a moment that I will comprehend everything in my life. I must trust in Him and have faith in His promises. You must do the same. Do not limit your ability to learn, lest you limit your ability to receive revelation and instruction from the Father.

"And if anyone thinks that he knows anything, he knows nothing yet as he ought to know," (1Corinthians 8:2 NKJV) When I stumbled upon this scripture, my own father's old saying came to mind......"the one thing a wise man knows is that he knows nothing at all." Once again we see here that we should not limit ourselves intellectually. As we look back on our lives we all see times when we should have listened to advice. Only you know the reason you chose not to take the advice. Maybe you were just being stubborn, maybe you were being proud. In either case, at the time you were convinced you were correct and ended up being wrong. So what you thought you knew, you did not know. My grandmother used to say, "Hindsight is 20/20." As a youngster I didn't really understand that saying, yet today I look upon it as some of the sagest advice I've ever received.

Open your eyes, your ears, your mind, and your heart so you can receive God's messages for you. Don't be shallow and miss potential blessings and teachings because of your biases and assumptions. If God used a bush to speak to Moses *(not to mention he used Moses who stuttered to lead the Israelites),* and a donkey to speak to Balaam; what can't He use to deliver His messages? Wasn't it a baby sent to an unwed mother in a manger that was used to save our souls? Don't judge the packaging, rather cherish the gift found within. In closing I would like to leave you with one scripture to meditate on..... ***"But the Lord said to Samuel, Do not look at his appearance or at his physical stature, because I have refused him. For the Lord does not see as man sees; for man looks at the outward appearance, but the Lord looks at the heart."*** (1Samuel 16:7)

BE BLESSED BE FAITHFUL

THE COMPANY WE KEEP

"Do not be unequally yoked with together with unbelievers. For what fellowship has righteousness with lawlessness? And what communion has light with darkness?"
(2 Corinthians 6:14 NKJV)

"Do not be deceived: Evil company corrupts good habits."
(1 Corinthians 15:33 NKJV)

"For we have spent enough of our past lifetime in doing the will of the Gentiles-when we walked in lewdness, lusts, drunkenness, revelries, drinking parties, and abominable idolatries. In regard to these, they think it strange that you do not run with them in the same flood of dissipation, speaking evil of you"
(1 Peter 4:3-4 NKJV)

I'd like to speak on a topic I'm sure you've received extensive guidance on since you were very young. The company you keep. I remember my parents would often tell me little sayings like, "Everyone you think is your friend is not your friend." "Everybody doesn't have your best interest in mind." "You keep running with that crowd, you gon' be guilty by association." I would be remiss if I left out the classic, "Birds of a feather flock together." Sound familiar? I'm sure it does. I'm sure I was like all of you and told my parents and elders all the excuses my little mind could think of. Usually I'd hit them with the, "You don't know them like I do." Or the classic, "Things are different then when you were my age, that's how we handle things." Looking back on our lives I'm sure we all see times when we should have applied those "simple' little sayings. Amazing how something so simple can hold so much weight, huh? How much heartache could we have been saved had we just followed these directions? Hmmmmm....

Well I'm here today to tell you, God feels the same way our parents did. He wants us to be careful who we associate with. He realizes how man's mind works, and how people will base their opinion of you on who you associate with. Deeper than that, he knows how easily influenced we are by our peers and surroundings. Throughout the scriptures he warns us to be careful of our relationships. Be they romantic, or platonic. ***"Do not be deceived: 'Evil Company corrupts good habits.'"*** (1 Corinthians 15:33). This short passage from 1 Corinthians speaks to the heart of our subject, "Evil company corrupts good habits." No matter how well intentioned you may start out, being around the wrong influences will knock you off track. How many times in life do you remember going in to a situation with the right intention? But somewhere between conception and execution it came out all wrong. Ever leave the house to perform a simple task, meet up with a friend, and find yourself in a world of trouble? That is what this text is referring to, those types of situations. See in a relationship (be it platonic or romantic) we take characteristics and habits from the other person. If you hang around someone who works out, either you'll begin exercising or they'll stop. Hang out with someone who drinks, eventually you'll begin drinking or they'll stop. Why is this? Because one's habits determine one's activities. If you make a habit of depending on the Lord for guidance, either those around you will follow suit or.....well let's not even speak that in to existence. AMEN?

    Let's go back to that old saying, "Birds of a feather flock together." There is a lot of truth in that statement. The Bible puts it another way, **_"Do not be unequally yoked with together with unbelievers. For what fellowship has righteousness with lawlessness? And what communion has light with darkness?"_** (2 Corinthians 6:14 NKJV) If your parents said it, what would make you think your heavenly Father wouldn't feel the same way? If you're living for Christ, what business do you have with someone who is not? You have nothing in common, you're not even headed in the same direction. So what is the purpose of the relationship? Let me help you, nothing positive. Now, I'm not saying that as believers we are not to witness to unbelievers. Lord knows, that is what spreading the Gospel is about. ***" When Jesus heard that, He said to them 'Those who are well have no need of a physician, but those who are sick.'"*** (Matthew 9:12 NKJV) Let's not take that out of context. I'm not saying give up on those around you who don't follow the word of God. I'm saying, how are you going to be able to stay strong in your walk, if you surround yourself with people who can't build you up?

Simply put, how can you learn to be a better boxer, unless you're around boxers and trainers? How can you be a better basketball player, unless your around basketball players and coaches? If I tell you I'm a Doctor, but when you come to the hospital I'm in a janitor uniform, what are you going to think? Don't hinder the strength of your ministry to others in any way you can control. The company you keep, is something you can control. I can tell you all day I'm a changed man, but if every time you see me I'm with the same old friends....have I really changed? We know that change in the Lord is complete, total. That doesn't mean we turn our backs on our old friends, we pray for them and hope that God will bring them to the truth as well. It also means we should be making new friends, who are engaged in activities which reflect our beliefs. 2 Corinthians 6:3 NKJV reads ***"We give no offense in anything, that our ministry may not be blamed."*** Once you become a child of God people are not just judging you anymore. Your actions don't just affect you, but the entire body of Christ. So please, be conscious that you're setting a good example in all you do.

Didn't you come to Christ because you wanted to make a change? I know for me, I was fed up with the life I was living. I knew that the way I was going, I was going to crash and burn. I found myself in a jail cell with nothing else to read but an "Our Daily Bread," crying out to God to take control of my life. To cleanse me, and show me His purpose and will for my life. *"For we have spent enough of our past lifetime in doing the will of the Gentiles-when we walked in lewdness, lusts, drunkenness, revelries, drinking parties, and abominable idolatries. In regard to these, they think it strange that you do not run with them in the same flood of dissipation, speaking evil of you."* (1Peter 4:3-4 NKJV)

Do you feel that way today? Then make that change, take Jesus into your heart and never look back. Philippians 3:13-14 (NKJV) reads, *"Brethren, I do not count myself to have apprehended; but one thing I do, forgetting those things which are behind and reaching forward to those things which are ahead, I press toward the goal for the prize of the upward call of God in Christ Jesus."* I'm not saying it will be easy, or that it will happen overnight. I'm simply saying press on for that prize family and don't give up. Your old "friends" may not understand, they may even call you everything but a child of God. Yet God will be there, and He'll provide you with new brothers and sisters in the faith. You never know, some of those old friends might decide to follow along. What a blessing that would be? Step out on faith, leave the past behind…..embrace the future.

BE BLESSED BE FAITHFUL

KNOW BETTER, DO BETTER!!!

"Therefore, to him who knows to do good and does not do it, to him it is sin."
(James 4:17 NKJV)

"For it would have been better for them not to have known the way of righteousness, than having known it, to turn from the holy commandment delivered to them."
(2 Peter 2:21 NKJV)

"For if we sin willfully after we have received the knowledge of the truth, there is no longer a sacrifice for sins, but a certain fearful expectation of judgement, and fiery indignation which will devour the adversaries."
(Hebrews 10:26-27 NKJV)

"As a dog returns to his own vomit, so a fool repeats his folly."
(Proverbs 26:11 NKJV)

Question, how many of you would quit a great job for a terrible one? Or who would trade good weather for bad? Let me be a little more direct....which of you would choose death over life? Any takers? LOL. I hope the answer is an emphatic **NO!** Unfortunately, many Christians do just this all the time. Trade in the eternal life and salvation they have to fulfill the temporary wants of this life. Often concessions are made and we willingly sin, taking advantage of God's grace....or so we think, remember; ***"Do not be deceived, God is not mocked; for whatever a man sows, that he will also reap."*** (Galatians 6:3 NKJV) While God forgives us of our sin, even to the point he doesn't remember them, there must be justice for our misdeeds. The question I pose is, why do we choose to do this to ourselves? Why do we take one step forward, then four backwards? Scripture states on many occasions that we should not do this. I've highlighted a few scriptures today to help us discuss this topic.

As a child we are often told what we can and can not do. Though we may have felt at the time as though our parents were trying to stop our fun, in hindsight *we* know it was just for our own good. This is much the same as our relationship with the Father. OK, I'll entertain the notion that the things of this world seem wonderful. Yet one day it will all come crashing to an end, and we'll regret we didn't heed His instructions. ***"Therefore, to him who knows to do good and does not do it, to him it is sin."*** (James 5:17 NKJV) It would be different if we hadn't been

Job 32:18

instructed not to do certain things. God is the epitome of justice, He would never hold us responsible for something we are unaware of. That is why He left clear instructions on how He wants us to live. The Bible is translated in to every language on the planet, missionaries abound, and there is no shortage of churches. So we have no excuses. John 15:22 (NKJV) reads, ***"If I had not came and spoken to them, they would have no sin, but now they have no excuse for their sin."*** For any of you who are unaware, that's some of those red letters. He loves us, he died for us .....he made sure we have no excuse when the end comes.

As I said before, it would be different if we didn't know what God expected of our lives. ***"And that servant who knew his master's will, and did not prepare himself or do according to his will, shall be beaten with many stripes. But he who did not know, yet committed things deserving of stripes, shall be beaten with few. For everyone to whom much is given, from him much will be required; and to whom much has been committed, of him thy will ask more."*** (Luke 12:47-48 NKJV) Once again, the above words are those of Jesus Himself. It's not that those who don't know the Gospel will not be judged, just that their punishment won't be as severe. As for those of us who know, how the hammer will fall on us. See in that passage it says, "to whom much is given, from him much will be required." I'm here to tell you we were given the Son of God, I'll let you determine how much is required. ***"For it would have***

been better for them not to have known the way of righteousness, than having known it, to turn from the holy commandment delivered to them." (2 Peter 2:21 NKJV) How true these words of Peter are. The next time you think it's o.k. to just do whatever you please, be mindful of the truth. God sees all, knows all, and **you** will have to answer to God as to why you disregarded his commandments. By the way, that guy who gave His life for you.....Jesus.....he'll be standing right there too.

"For if we sin willfully after we have received the knowledge of the truth, there no longer remains a sacrifice for sins, but a certain fearful expectation of judgment, and fiery indignation which will devour the adversaries." (Hebrews 10:26-27 NKJV) Now that's a powerful passage there! Makes you want to walk the straight and narrow! Yes it means exactly what it says. I know there are a few of you going in to your prayer closets right now. AMEN. But let's break it down, just for those who may not realize the true meaning of this passage. ***"For if we sin willfully after we have received the knowledge of the truth,"*** That's talking to you. You who just yesterday was talking bad about your neighbor....you who left church and cursed out that driver on the road....you who just last week told that "little white lie." In fact there isn't one of us "Christians" who doesn't fall in to this category. (Boy, I don't know about you, but I appreciate grace more day by day!) The next phrase is, ***"there is no longer a sacrifice for sins."*** Jesus has already been crucified once for our sins. The next time He comes back, it will be to **judge** us all. Which leads to the next statement. ....*" but a certain fearful expectation of judgment, and fiery indignation which will devour the adversaries."* Whoooo! That's right, on that great day of judgment, all who aren't in His will are adversaries. We should not deceive ourselves, not for one minute that we will not be devoured. All these years of Bible study, Sunday school, Vacation Bible School, church services, revivals and the like means we are well aware of the judgment that awaits the ungodly.

I know the trials of life can get us down. It's always easier to revert back to old habits of survival when things get tough. Just know that God puts us through trials to test and strengthen our faith. *"For I consider that the sufferings of this present time are not worthy to be compared with the glory which shall be revealed in us." (Romans 8:18 NKJV)* I beg you to hold on to the promises God has left with us. I plead that you focus on your eternal soul rather than your temporal existence. Be wise in the knowledge that God will never forsake you, and that He has given you the strength to make it through. *"As a dog returns to his own vomit, So a fool repeats his folly."* (Proverbs 26:11 (NKJV) Let none of you fall in to this category. Do not return to your former ways, but hold fast to the new person God has made you to be. Why trade in a pair of brand new shoes for an old pair of beat up ones? Doesn't make any sense. Neither does going back to who you were before you knew the goodness of God.

BE BLESSED BE FAITHFUL

Job 32:18

GOT FEAR???

"For God has not given us a spirit of fear, but of power and of love and of a sound mind."
(2 Timothy 1:7 NKJV)

"The fear of man brings a snare, But whoever trusts in the Lord shall be safe."
(Proverbs 29:25 NKJV)

"What then shall we say to these things? If God is for us, who can be against us?"
(Romans 8:31 NKJV)

"There is no fear in love; but perfect love casts out fear, because fear involves torment. But he who fears has not been made perfect in love."
(1 John 4:18 NKJV)

"In God I have put my trust; I will not be afraid. What can man do to me?"
(Psalms 56:11 NKJV)

What do you fear in life? No need to "act" invincible, what do you fear? Is it financial stability, your husband or wife leaving you? Do you fear you will lose a friendship because you've chosen to follow Christ? Do you fear your children will resent you and not speak to you because you discipline them? There are even smaller fears. Simple fears like, "Do these shoes match this outfit?" Think about it for a second, and ask yourself, "What do I fear?"

Fear is perfectly "natural." It is an emotion we all experience at some time and point. Don't be ashamed of it, rather analyze the catalyst of your fear and deal with it. Most fears we can't deal with so we need to go to the Father and draw on His strength. Our first text tells us, ***"For God has not given us a spirit of fear, but of power and of love and of a sound mind."*** (2 Timothy 1:7) So if we are led by His spirit, and allow His spirit to guide us, we should not fear. We know that this emotion should not occupy the same place the Spirit of the Father does. That is not to say we will not have reservations in life, or be cautious. It is saying that no matter the situation you should be confident and empowered. Romans 8:37-39 (NKJV) reads, ***"Yet in all these things we are more than conquerors through Him who loved us. For I am persuaded that neither death nor life, nor angels nor principalities nor powers, nor things present or things to come, nor height nor depth, nor any other created thing, shall be able to separate us from the love of God which is in Christ Jesus our Lord."*** There it is again, that word love. We know that God is love, correct? This passage in Romans confirms the attitude we need to take with all situations in life. Not one of fear, but one of a conqueror, because of the love He has for us. Let's analyze this love aspect a little further.

"There is no fear in love; but perfect love casts out fear, because fear involves torment. But he who fears has not been made perfect in love." (1 John 4:18 NKJV) That scripture is pretty straightforward, yet how many times have we read it and really not made it a part of our lives. There is no fear in love, which means there is no fear in God and we have been reborn in His image. So how can there be any fear in us? Perfect love casts out fear, that perfect love is God. So if you have God in you, any fear you sense is an illusion. The last sentence clearly states that... "he who fears has not been made perfect in love." Ask yourself, have you been made perfect in love? Have you truly let God take the reins in your life, strengthen your infirmities, and PERFECT who you are? If you're living in fear of the economy, your spouse, your in-laws, your boss, or anything....you ought to meditate on this verse. Let me say it again, there is no fear **IF** you have God.....and trust in God.

I hope no one is taking this offensively. Saying, "I know he didn't just tell me I don't have God in my life because I have fear." "He got a lot of nerve, as if he's never feared anything!" "Who made him judge and jury, my Mama told me a little fear is healthy." For the record, yes, I have had fears. No, I am not perfect. I do not condemn anyone right now reading this who may be struggling with fear. Rather, I am here to encourage you and help you overcome. Often in life we say we fear things, when in actuality we just lack confidence in a given area. Take the time to really analyze what you are feeling, so that you can deal with it appropriately. If you go to the doctor and say your foot hurts, and it's really your ankle how do you ever expect a proper diagnosis? AMEN? Same thing with your spiritual life. If you say something is the problem, that's what you'll work on and you may live the rest of your life never treating the true problem.

    I personally feel fearing anything other than God is taking away from His true place in your life. Only God has absolute power, everything in this world is created by man so it will perish. The power in the things of this world is temporary, vain, and usually blown out of proportion. When we allow things of this world to place that type of fear in us, we are essentially giving them the power of God in our lives. How? We allow those things to direct how we look, where we go, our expectations, every aspect of our life. We allow those false powers to direct us in ways that only, you guessed it, GOD SHOULD! ***"The fear of man brings a snare, But whoever trusts in the Lord shall be safe."*** (Proverbs 29:25 NKJV) Fearing these mortal issues in life only hinder us from accomplishing God's mission for us in this world. Essentially robbing us of the blessings and riches He has in store for us in return for being obedient to His word.

Do not be robbed of your calling and blessings. Rather be encouraged, and empowered by the promises of our heavenly Father. When adversity and hardships come your way stand on Romans 8:31 (NKJV), *"What then shall we say to these things? If God is for us, who can be against us?"* Oh, how glorious is that passage? The reassurance it gives us when faced with this world's "fears." These illusions, used by the master of illusion of himself, Satan, trying to deceive God's people. **DO NOT BE DECEIVED!** Rather arm yourself daily with the word of God, so that you can fight these emotions in your mind and lives of your loved ones. The next time fear comes knocking at your door, boldly cast it out of your life in the name of Jesus. AMEN? Amen indeed.

I want to leave you today with one last scripture to remind you never to be fearful, *"In God I have put my trust; I will not be afraid. What can man do to me?"* (Psalms 56:11 NKJV) Say it with me...."In God I have put my trust." Not in man, not in money, not in a weapon. Just in God, and God alone. **"I will not be afraid!!!!"** That is a statement, a bold statement, removing any question that fear has a hold on you. **"What can man do to me?"** Nothing, not now, and not ever. Repeat this scripture as often as you need, to remind yourself why you don't have any fear. If you have not put all your trust in God, what are you waiting for? Take that step now. Put your trust in the One who will never let you down, never disappoint you, never abandon you, and never use man's "scare" tactics. Do it today, why spend another day in fear of life's lies? ***"And do not fear those who kill the body but cannot kill the soul. But rather fear Him who is able to destroy both soul and body in hell."*** (Matthew 10:28 NKJV) Place your fear in the One who controls life and death, not in those things who don't even have power over themselves. AMEN!!!

"The fear of the Lord is the beginning of knowledge, but fools despise wisdom and instruction." (Proverbs 1:7 NKJV) Fear God, put your trust in His word and have knowledge. The knowledge that tells you, amongst a host of other things, there is nothing to fear. The devil is a liar, and he always will be. You have to make the decision not to allow him, and his tool fear to have power in your life. Make that decision now, not tomorrow, not in a few minutes, but right now.

BE BLESSED BE FAITHFUL

TRUE POWER

"For the kingdom of God is not in word but in power."
(1 Corinthians 4:20 NKJV)

"But you shall receive power when the Holy Spirit has come upon you; and you shall be witnesses to Me in Jerusalem, and in all Judea and Samaria, and to the end of the earth."
(Acts 1:8 NKJV)

"And He said to me, 'My grace is sufficient for you, for My strength is made perfect in weakness.' Therefore most gladly I will rather boast in my infirmities, that the power of Christ may rest upon me."
(2 Corinthians 12:9 NKJV)

"God is my strength and power, and he makes my way perfect."
(2 Samuel 22:33 NKJV)

"He gives power to the weak, and to those who have no might He increases strength."

(Isaiah 40:29 NKJV)

"But truly I am full of power by the Spirit of the Lord, and of justice and might, to declare to Jacob his transgression and Israel his sin. (Micah 3:8 NKJV)

"For our gospel did not come to you in word only, but also in power, and in the Holy Spirit and in much assurance, as you know what kind of men we were among you for your sake."
(1 Thessalonians 1:5 NKJV)

Job 32:18

People live for it, die for it, dedicate their lives to it, and ruin their lives in the pursuit of it. It is the ultimate achievement, nothing on earth can top the allure it holds. **_POWER!!!!_** Pure and unadulterated. Since childhood all of our heroes have exuded this quality. As teenagers the people we most admire display it. As adults, it seems most of us are on a quest to achieve it. We pursue education with the hope we will receive a high paying job, so that one day we will be the **employer** and not the **employee.** It is a shame we don't take the time out to enjoy the process of learning, don't you agree? There are countless other facets of life where we miss the true value of the experience because we're focused on the end result Most times that end result is not God's glory, but our own ascension to power. However little or great, this is how many of us equate our value. Yet once we get to the top of the mountain, why aren't we feel fulfilled? Why is it that what we have pursued so vehemently really gives us no sense of gratification? Sorry to disappoint you, but we can **never** achieve any true power on our own. Scripture shows us the source of all things, especially the source of true power in this world.

    The difference between when we say something, and when God says it is pretty simple. Nine out of ten we don't mean it, and every time He says it....you can count on it. God spoke the earth and all of the treasures within it in to existence. **_"For the kingdom of God is not in word but in power."_** (1 Corinthians 4:20 NKJV) Do not be deceived when God speaks it is not just words, they are always backed with action. Actions which display the sovereign power He and He alone controls. This same power is also at our disposal as His children. We know that we have the indwelling of the Holy Spirit giving us access to His power. The power to cast out demons in our lives and the lives of those we love. The power to heal the sick, the power to any and everything He wills necessary. The bible is a tool of empowerment, to make us aware of what is truly being given to us. Are you drawing on the power?

When Jesus was preparing to leave the disciples, He informed them that God would provide a Comforter. Someone to assist them in spreading the Word, and giving them the ability to perform the same miracles He himself performed. After returning for 40 days and appearing to over 500 people, God makes known what exactly the disciples would receive from the Comforter. ***"But you shall receive power when the Holy Spirit has come upon you; and you shall be witnesses to Me in Jerusalem, and in all Judea and Samaria, and to the end of the earth."*** (Acts 1:8 NKJV) Do you see it, "But you shall receive <u>power</u> when the Holy Spirit has come upon you...." Prior to this point the disciples were just ordinary men, with an extraordinary friend who could do many great things. Yet now the promise Jesus had made was being made manifest, ***"Most assuredly, I say to you, he who believes in Me, the works that I do he will do also; and greater works than these he will do,***

because I go to My Father." (John 14:12 NKJV) The ability to do these works is a power that they received once the Holy Spirit came upon them. In layman's terms: the disciples were knowledgeable and had done some great works. Yet it would not be until <u>God gave them power</u> that the true nature of their abilities would be revealed.

The same is true for each of us. Naturally we are all gifted, and certain aspects of life come to us quite easily. Some are great artists, others good with finances, some excellent speakers, others still are even naturally wise. Understand though, we will never know the true depth of our abilities until God reveals it to us. Until we go to Him and allow Him to show us how to properly utilize these gifts. ***"And He said to me, 'My grace is sufficient for you, for My strength is made perfect in weakness.' Therefore most gladly I will rather boast in my infirmities, that the power of Christ may rest upon me."*** (2 Corinthians 12:9 NKJV) Here Paul is speaking about the thorn in his flesh which He'd asked God to remove. God's reply is, "My *grace is sufficient for you, for My strength is made perfect in weakness."* Essentially what God's saying is, our weaknesses are when His strength can truly be recognized. See, where we believe we have strength at never go to Him. Yet where we're weak we run to Him and allow Him the opportunity to make His strength known. How much more strength and power would we have in those areas of our life we think we have power in, if we did the same in those areas as we do in the ones where we know we are weak? That is what the last piece of this text is attesting to, *"Therefore most gladly I will rather boast in my infirmities, that the power of Christ may rest upon me."* Paul is basically saying he would rather make known his weaknesses, so that God is glorified in his life. So that others can see the power bestowed upon him by God. Isn't that how we should all be? Humble in all our ways, always giving God the glory for being the source of our true .power.

    I'm often asked, "What makes you think people will actually read your sermons?" "Why do you think anyone would pay heed to the words of an incarcerated felon?" Well Micah 3:8 (NKJV) reads ***"But truly I am full of power by the Spirit of the Lord, and of justice and might, to declare to Jacob his transgression and Israel his sin."*** Does that answer the questions and naysayers? We must all harness this power God has given us to spread His word. We have all been given a ministry that can do mighty works, as long as it is lead by and powered by the Holy Spirit. No power on earth can hope to oppose it, let alone stop it. Now that's real power, isn't that what you really want? ***"For our gospel did not come to you in word only, but also in power, and in the Holy Spirit and in much assurance, as you know what kind of men we were among you for your sake."*** (1 Thessalonians 1:5 NKJV) That is what will happen when you begin utilizing the power God has placed within you. You will realize the insignificance of the power you sought. People will not only hear the gospel you preach, but they will see the power it has in your life. Then that same power will begin to affect the lives of others; changing them, and molding them into their true selves. Slowly but surely, the world will begin to rectify it's definition of power. We will re-evaluate those whom we associate as powerful. Eventually we will come to the realization that humans have no power, accept for what God allows them to use.

My brothers and sisters if you truly want power, submit all of yourself to God. To receive the power you seek, you must surrender the power you 'think" you possess. You must give God the honor and glory in all things, then He will give you power to carry out His will for your life. He will provide you with strength to deal with all the opposition you will face. Then those who have been given eyes to see will have a chance to witness real power……<u>the power of</u> **<u>GOD!!!</u>**

<u>BE BLESSED BE FAITHFUL</u>

ARE YOU TUNED IN?

"They are of the world. Therefore they speak as of the world, and the world hears them. We are of God. He who knows God hears us; he who is not of God does not hear us. By this we know the spirit of truth and the spirit of error." (1 John 4:5-6 NKJV)

"For the message of the cross is foolishness to those who are perishing, but to us who are being saved it is the power of God." (1 Corinthians 1:18 NKJV)

"He who comes from above is above all,; he who is of the earth is earthly and speaks of the earth. He who comes from heaven is above all." (John 3:31 NKJV)

"But the natural man does not receive the things of the Spirit of God, for they are foolishness to him; nor can he know them, because they are spiritually discerned." (1 Corinthians 2:14 NKJV)

Job 32:18

"But even if our gospel is veiled, it is veiled to those who are perishing, whose minds the god of this age has blinded, who do not believe, lest the light of the gospel of the glory of Christ, who is the image of God, should shine on them."
(2 Corinthians 4:3-4 NKJV)

How many of you, before you were saved, remember those "Jesus freaks?" Oh, don't front, you remember them. Those "fanatical" people you would come across who always wanted to talk about the "good news." We all know the "Ned Flanders" of the world. Wouldn't it always be at what seemed to be the most inopportune times too? Like when you were headed in 7-11 to grab a case of beer, or some cigars. Maybe you were in the CVS picking up some condoms or an EPT. Somebody out there knows what I'm talking about. I remember I would always walk away asking myself, "What makes them act like that?" I know I would look at the news, and things didn't look to good to me. The economy was failing, children starving all over the place, and the cat that owes me that money is still ducking me. LOL. Can you relate? I know you can. Looking back, I can completely understand. Now I must admit though….. **I IS A JESUS FREAK!!!!!** And I'm sooooo proud to say it, aren't you? Well friends that is precisely what I want to talk about. What makes a person want to witness no matter the situation? What makes a Jesus freak so adamant and energetic all the time?

Our first text today is ***"But the natural man does not receive the things of the Spirit of God, for they are foolishness to him; nor can he know them, because they are spiritually discerned."*** (1 Corinthians 2:14 NKJV) This tells us why we didn't understand those "Jesus Freaks." We were not living in the Spirit so we couldn't comprehend the fruit of the Spirit. We couldn't comprehend the fruit of the Spirit,

Job 32:18

because we were separated from God who is the only way to receive spiritual discernment. So of course it looked foolish to us, because we were looking through our carnal eyes. Not the spiritual glasses He gives us to correct our vision. How does a person have joy, when they have a terminal disease? How can a man smile, when his employer tells him he's a victim of "corporate downsizing?" Because they have God, and they know that's all we truly need. They have placed their trust in Him, and have received the comfort that is only given by Him. ***"For the message of the cross is foolishness to those who are perishing, but to us who are being saved it is the power of God."*** (1 Corinthians 1:18 NKJV) If you have not submitted to His will and purpose how could you possibly understand the benefits of it? Still struggling with this concept? Allow me to approach it another way. If you've never skydived, how can you know the "rush" associated with the experience? You can't. The same is true in relation to things of the Spirit.

When we were caught up in our own ambitions it seemed completely ludicrous to do many of the things we do now. Take for instance sacrificing a beautiful Saturday to feed the homeless, .when we could be out having a barbecue. I remember wondering why my Mother would buy presents for other people when we barely had any ourselves. Or how she would invite people to come by and eat when we were struggling ourselves. She would always say, "God gave it to us, so we can give it to other people." In my mind I would say, "No, God gave it to us because he know we hungry 'round here!" LOL. "Maybe if they did some more praying, and went to church more often, they'd have some food too." I wasn't always saved either, so trust me I know the thoughts that can come to one's mind. Somebody needs to be saying AMEN because they were the same way. LOL. "

They are of the world. Therefore they speak as of the world, and the world hears them. We are of God. He who knows God hears us; he who is not of God does not hear us. By this we know the spirit of truth and the spirit of error." (1 John 4:5-6 NKJV) Here in 1st John is the answer to those questions that were in my little mind. I was still in the world so I couldn't understand the ways of God. Yet my mother and many others could so the incomprehensible made complete sense to them. Now that we are believers we to grasp this concept. I want to highlight the last sentence of the text though, *"By this we know the spirit of truth and the spirit of error."* As you witness about God's mercy and goodness in your life, it reveals to you His children from the worldly. We can discern those who have accepted the truth of Christ Jesus, and those who are still living in the error of the world and its ways. Getting a better understanding of the "Jesus Freak" syndrome? Great, let's keep on plowing through.

As I said before, I am happy to label myself a "Jesus Freak." I am not ashamed to spread the Word of God and witness to others what he has, and continues to do in my life. People may not understand, but that is not my concern. I'm so thankful for what He has done I'm not able to contain it. I must tell someone else, I'm compelled to. Oh, I know I'm not the only one who feels this way. Is their a witness? He's been so good to me; I feel the only way I can show my appreciation is to tell everybody about it!

"But even if our gospel is veiled, it is veiled to those who are perishing, whose minds the god of this age has blinded, who do not believe, lest the light of the gospel of the glory of Christ, who is the image of God, should shine on them." (2 Corinthians 4:3-4 NKJV) Those who don't understand have not accepted the eternal life that is in Christ Jesus. It is my hope, because it is the Father's hope, that through us as believers they may also come to Him and be healed. That their eyes may be opened, and they accept this salvation being offered to them.

"He who comes from above is above all; he who is of the earth is earthly and speaks of the earth. He who comes from heaven is above all." (John 3:31 NKJV) Brothers and sisters this statement refers to Jesus himself. Yet, through your adoption in to God's family, it also includes you. You have been reborn, and the Spirit which is in you is heavenly. Therefore, your attitude and perception is going to be "tuned in" to that which is heavenly. It's just like a radio station, if your not tuned to the right frequency....you can't tune in to the program. Before we were saved we were tuned in to the wrong frequency and couldn't hear what those "Jesus Freaks" were hearing. Now that we've finally tuned in, were in perfect unison with them. What a joyous feeling to know that we are on one accord with the Father? Isn't that what life is all about? Isn't that the whole reason why Jesus gave His life on the Cross? So the next time somebody calls you a "Jesus Freak," or looks at you strangely because you're in the Spirit…..pray for them….. witness to them. And rejoice that you're tuned in to WGOD… the station of truth.

BE BLESSED BE FAITHFUL

GOD EVERYWHERE

"Then the servants of the king of Syria said to him, 'Their gods are gods of the hills. Therefore they were stronger than we; but if we fight against them in the plain, surely we will be stronger than they."
(1 Kings 20:23 NKJV)

"Then a man of God came and spoke to the king of Israel, and said, Thus says the Lord: Because the Syrians have said, "The Lord is God of the hills, but He is not God of the valleys, "therefore I will deliver all this great multitude into your hand, and you shall know that I am the Lord."
(1 Kings 20:28 NKJV)

How often in our lives do we look at those doing well and say; "My God is truly awesome, blessing those He loves." "Look at their house, their clothes, their cars, only God could bless someone like that." "You know, she's always doing outreach work at the church, that's why God always makes sure she has the newest outfits and hats!" "Look at that suit, God is blessing him." The list goes on, and I'm sure you've heard them all of your life. I do believe that God blesses some of us with large amounts of material wealth and success. I'm a firm believer that he provides abundantly for all of our needs. That is not up for debate. My question is, why don't we say someone is blessed when their down? Why is it we don't see God's hand in the "valleys" of our lives and others? 2Corinthians 10:7 (NKJV) reads, ***"Do you look at things according to the outward appearance? If any one is convinced in himself that he is Christ's, let him again consider this in himself, that just as he is Christ's, even so we are Christ's."*** This is true and we're sure of it. Since we know God and Christ are one, then we know we are also one with the Father through Christ. So why then would we think that for some reason or another, this is not true in the "valleys" of life?

In the scripture reading today, we see an practical illustration of this situation. The Syrians had convinced themselves that the God of Israel only resided in the hills, or "high places." Therefore they could claim victory against the children of Israel if they fought them in the valleys (low places). How true is this fact in our own lives? How many of us have become "spiritual Syrians" in our walk. Often only seeing God's power and majesty in the "high places," not recognizing Him in the "low places" of our lives. Through not recognizing Him in our low places we leave ourselves open to attack, and defeat by the enemy. If you notice the Syrians looked at the valleys as the most opportune time to attack the Israelites. Satan uses a similar tactic in our own lives.

We all have those so called, "friends." AMEN? The ones who tell you something is too hard, or unachievable in our current conditions. Telling us we need to lower our goals and outlooks, be more "realistic." The ones who say, "Had you gone to church, these things wouldn't be happening." Who say, "God isn't blessing your for this reason and that reason." Or, "God has turned His back on you for this reason and that reason." Well it clearly reads in scripture; ***"Be strong and of good courage, do not fear nor be afraid of them; for the Lord Your God, He is the One who goes with you. He will not leave you nor forsake you."*** *(Deuteronomy 31:6 NKJV)* Jesus then reassures us; **"teaching them to observe all things that I commanded you; and lo, I am with you always, even to the end of the age."** (Matthew 28:20 NKJV) So we know abandoning us is just not in His plans.

Did it ever dawn on any of these "spiritual Syrians" that God set up these circumstances to show His power? To show that He is everywhere, that He can pull us up out of any situation. Did it ever dawn on any of them that God could be using your circumstances as a test of faith? The scripture in Deuteronomy says; *"Be strong and of good courage, do not fear nor be afraid of them;....."*. Does that say anything about giving up when things get tough? No, it sounds like words to encourage us to go in to any situation, with a victorious mind state. AMEN? The next part of the scripture reads *"....for the Lord your God, He is the One who goes with you. He will not leave you nor forsake you."* Does that sound like he abandons us? Ever? Sounds more like the exact opposite doesn't it?

Oh my people, don't let others deceive you of God's intentions and plans. You **MUST** study His word, so you can **KNOW** what he plans for us. How often do we lose hope, because we listen to another person's opinion? Don't let anyone steal your joy with their ignorance, or due to your own. That is why the scripture tells us, ***"Be diligent to present yourself approved to God, a worker who does not need to be ashamed, rightly dividing the word of truth,"*** (2 Timothy 2:16) AMEN? Don't fall for the enemy's lies and traps. Don't be deceived in the "valleys of life."

The second scripture for ends with, *".....therefore I will deliver all this great multitude into your hand, and you shall know that I am the Lord."* Once again, God is guaranteeing victory for His people. No matter what the number of adversaries. He says; *"I will deliver this great multitude into your hand..."* So what does that tell you? No matter what circumstances are affecting your life, He can and will pull you through. So why let others opinions sway you from His promise? Hold fast, go through the hard times with the mind of a conqueror, not as a victim. The scripture goes on to say;*" and you shall know that I am the Lord."* AMEN? *"....and **you** shall know that I am the **LORD**.* Notice it wasn't for the Syrians, it was for the Israelites to know His power. He pulls us through these valleys so that we, His children can recognize His majesty. Not so others will, but for us to know. He's not concerned withf anyone else recognizing it, just you. He loves us so much, He never wants us to think He's not with us. So in the midst of all these people saying He's turned His back, they may even say that another "circumstance" pulled you out of your situation. Yet <u>you</u> know who actually did it, so <u>you</u> give Him the praise, let the world know what He's done in your life. Have you? Are you?

    See the same God there with you in the pew on Sunday, is the same God with you at the bar stool on Friday. The same God that was there when you got that promotion, is the same One comforting you when the recession took away your job. The same God you praised when you were on top, is the same One you need to seek when times get tough. When people say that God is not with you, you tell them;, "No, He's here, I just wasn't seeking Him the way I should be." You defend your Father the same way He defends you. In those valleys of your life, praise him for the blessings. In those high points of your life, bless those in the valleys of life.

Aren't you glad we serve a God of everywhere, and every thing. There is nothing, no situation you are in, He can't pull you through. Greater than that, there is no thing or situation he doesn't **WANT** to pull you through. He just requires that we seek Him, and give **HIM** the praise. Not our own intellect, not the government fixing the economy, not the lotto, not our spouses and friends. Give your praise to Him, wouldn't you agree…..He's worthy? I'm so glad He came and found me in the valley of my life. I'm so glad He gave me victory when the odds were stacked against me. If you are give Him some praise. Let your life be praise for his goodness, ***"I beseech you therefore, brethren, by the mercies of God that you present your bodies a living sacrifice, holy, acceptable to God, which is your reasonable service. And do not be conformed to this world, but be transformed by the renewing of your mind, that you may prove what is that good and acceptable and perfect will of God."*** (Romans 12:1-2 NKJV)

From now on when you see somebody down don't assume that God isn't in their lives. Pray that the Lord is in their lives, offer an encouraging word, and let them know the valleys the Lord has pulled you out of. Let them know that the Lord is with them in their valley and He will give them the victory. Don't get pulled out of your valleys and become a "spiritual Syrians." Remember your time in the valleys, so you can remember how He brought you through. Remember those in the valleys, because He does.

Job 32:18

I know there's someone going through a valley right now in their lives, and I want to encourage you, troubles don't last always. In Psalms it reads, **_"For his anger is but for a moment, His favor is for life; Weeping may endure for a night, But joy comes in the morning."_** (Psalms 30:5 NKJV) Yes, he gets angry and disappointed with us. Don't we get angry and disappointed with ourselves? Yet, that is only for a short while. The time we spend in His good graces far exceeds the short time we may feel we are out of it. Don't let anyone ever tell you, and never believe, God is only there in the "hills" of our lives. Be secure in the fact that He is most assuredly there in the "valleys", leading you to victory. Not for anyone else, but for you to know that He is your Lord. Times in the valley are a time for us to reflect and be reminded of how deep His devotion to us is. See you in the valleys. Ill be the one with a smile on his face singing and dancing.

BE BLESSED BE FAITHFUL

THE BEST THINGS IN LIFE ARE FREE !!!

"For by grace you have been saved through faith, and that not of yourselves; it is the gift of God, not of works, lest anyone should boast."
(Ephesians 2:8-9 NKJV)

"And if by grace, then it is no longer of works; otherwise grace is no longer grace. But if it is of works, it is no longer grace; otherwise work is no longer work."
(Romans 11:6 NKJV)

"For the law was given through Moses, but grace and truth came through Jesus Christ."
(John 1:17 NKJV)

"But to each one of us grace was given according to the measure of Christ's gift."
(Ephesians 4:7 NKJV)

"For the Lord God is a sun and shield; The Lord will give grace and glory; no good

thing will He withhold from those who walk uprightly."
(Psalms 84:11 NKJV)

"For all have sinned and fall short of the glory of God, being justified freely by His grace through the redemption that is in Christ Jesus,"
(Romans 3:23-24 NKJV)

Greetings brothers and sisters! After writing on the subject of forgiveness, I felt compelled to follow it up with addressing the topic of **GRACE**. Now I'm not talking about that nice woman you know, or what you say before you eat a meal. No, I'm talking about the grace which allows you to be redeemed. Interestingly enough many believers often speak about grace yet when asked to define it they rarely can. Fear not, for with the assistance of the Holy Spirit, some light shall be shed on this subject. AMEN?

Let's first understand that grace is a gift. That's right brothers and sisters, there is nothing one can do to receive grace, it is freely given to us by the Father. Yet there is much *we* can do to show our appreciation for this gift, which we will touch upon later. ***"For by grace you have been saved through faith, and that not of yourselves; it is the gift of God, not of works, lest anyone should boast."*** (Ephesians 2:8-9 NKJV) This passage in Ephesians is pretty straightforward, yet many a Christian has never taken the time to really embrace its true meaning. The first statement, *"For by grace you have been saved through faith",* tells you the undeniable need for grace. It explains to you that without it you wouldn't even be able to have faith, let alone the salvation it brings. So not only is grace a gift but even the faith you exercise. God has designed it this way so He receives the glory in your salvation. The statement, *"it is the gift of God, not of works, lest anyone should boast"* tells you this. We as humans have done nothing to deserv, or earn the grace He has imparted on us. God has given us grace freely because of His love for us. This gift was bestowed upon mankind through the life of Jesus Christ. That is the significance of this passage, *"For the law was given through Moses, but grace and truth came through Jesus Christ."* (John 1:17 NKJV) God didn't charge us anything to receive His grace. Before mankind was aware we would even need it, He had already provided it. Here in the first chapter of John we see that truth also came through Christ. That truth is the Gospel. Pretty priceless gift too wouldn't you say?

    Now that we understand the concept of grace, that it is a gift, let's delve a little deeper. ***"And if by grace, then it is no longer of works; otherwise grace is no longer grace. But if it is of works, it is no longer grace; otherwise work is no longer work."*** (Romans 11:6 NKJV) As we live our lives, we must remember that we can not earn grace. Some of us think that through good works grace can be awarded to us, this is incorrect as this passage tells us. To work for grace would nullify the need for it. It would also devalue God's love for us. As believers we need to spread this message and stop the "mis-education" of our brothers and sisters. How many Christians lay awake at night filled with anxiety wondering if they're in God's good graces? Once again, it is critical that each of us **study** the Word so we are not deceived. A lot of misconceptions believers deal with could be eradicated if they followed this simple rule. Do not depend on another's knowledge of the Word…. study for your self.

Sorry about that, let me get back on track. ***"But to each one of us grace was given according to the measure of Christ's gift."*** (Ephesians 4:7 NKJV) This passage of scripture ensures that the grace we have received is abundant. It says that it *"was given according to the measure of Christ's gift"* My beloved, everything about Christ is eternal. That infers that the measurement of the gift is eternal. So if mercy was given "according to that measure," wouldn't it mean it is also eternal? AMEN? Go ahead, smile tell the person sitting next to you God's grace is eternal. Does that make you feel special? It should, because that He wants you to feel special.

Now that we understand grace is a gift, and we don't have to work for it let's examine **WHY** we have grace; ***"for all have sinned and fall short of the glory of God, being justified freely by His grace through the redemption that is in Christ Jesus,"*** (Romans 3:23-24 NKJV) We have grace because we have a sinful nature. I'm assuming all of you understand God's issue with sin so I won't get into that right now. (If you have any questions, I'd be more than happy to sit down and explain it to you.) Due to sin, man was hopelessly separated from God with no way to make amends. We could in no way make ourselves acceptable in His sight, so all of us were destined for eternal death. Yet our Father loves us, and He did not create us to be separated from Him. Enter Jesus Christ. Don't you just love J.C.? Yeah.. .he's my homeboy too.

Christ had to die for our sins so we could receive the gift of grace. God had to come in to our presence in order to deliver this most needed gift. Since there was no way for us to earn it, in order to bring us back into His presence He had to bestow grace on us to redeem us into His family. I know how you feel. When you think about all He's done for us, how could a person deny His existence? How could a person deny his love for us? How could a person deny His grace?

As with all things in regard to the Father, there is a requirement to receive His grace. Obedience my friends, obedience. ***"For the Lord God is a sun and shield; The Lord will give grace and glory; no good thing will He withhold from those who walk uprightly."*** (Psalms 84:11 NKJV) In order to accept His grace, you must walk in the way He has ordained us too. You must adhere to the precepts He has set forth. Did your parents ever give you a gift for being disobedient? Of course not. Why would God be any different? Okay, I can hear some of you now; ."but didn't you just say we can't do anything to receive grace?" Yes I did, there is nothing you can do to receive grace, but there is something you must do in order for it to be given to you. Notice it says, *"The Lord will give grace and glory no good thing will He withhold from those who walk uprightly."* That means that He does withhold grace from the disobedient. Understand?

How can I put this so I'm sure you understand it? Let's say hypothetically, I'm giving away new cars.

Hypothetically now, y'all know I'm in no position at this time to do as such. Now these cars are top of the line, kitted out, power everything, leather seats, I'm talking about draped up and dripped out. Ya dig? Yet I can't give you one if you don't have a license. Understand now? The car is free, but you need to fit a certain requirement to receive it. The same thing applies to grace. It is free, but you must be living righteously in order to truly receive it. There's no need in God bestowing grace on you, and you have not chosen to live righteously. You won't be able to appreciate the effect of grace otherwise. Got it?

I want each of you to go to the Father in prayer and thank Him for His grace. Not just the grace He has extended to you, but that He extends to all. Pray that He places you in positions where you can let His grace flow through you, so it can be extended to others. God means for us to share His grace, just as much as He wants us to share His love. Remember when you feel yourself caught up in the hustle and bustle of life.....the best things in life are free. Then **SMILE.** He'll be smiling with you.

BE BLESSED BE FAITHFUL

SPREAD THE WORD

"And since we have the same spirit of faith, according to what is written 'I believed and therefore I spoke' we also believe and therefore speak."
(2 Corinthians 4:13 NKJV)

"Him we preach, warning every man and teaching every man in all wisdom , that we may present every man perfect in Christ Jesus."
(Colossians 1:28 NKJV)

"Preach the word! Be ready in season and out of season. Convince, rebuke, exhort, with all longsuffering and teaching. For the time will come when they will not endure sound doctrine, but according to their own desires, because they have itching ears, they will heap up for themselves teachers; and they will turn their ears from the truth, and be turned to fables. But you be watchful in all things, endure afflictions, do the work of an evangelist, fulfill your ministry."
(2 Timothy 4:2-5 NKJV)

"For if I preach the gospel, I have nothing to boast of, for necessity is laid upon me; yes, woe is me if I do not preach the gospel!"
(1 Corinthians 9:16 NKJV)

"Go therefore and make disciples of all the nations, baptizing them in the name of the Father and of the Son and of the Holy Spirit, teaching them to observe all things that I have commanded you; and lo, I am with you always even to the end of the age, Amen"
(Matthew 28:19-20 NKJV)

Job 32:18

All the Bible scholars out there should be well acquainted with this passage. Here, Jesus gives the disciples there instructions and duties. It is known as the "Great Commission". Though these words were said to the 11 remaining disciples, but they were meant for all of us. It is God's will that all of us, as followers, spread the Gospel at every opportunity.....to all people; "....*make disciples of all the nations.*" I do believe the best way to spread that message is through the lives we lead, yet the power of God's Words is undeniably the greatest tool we can use. It is essential we preach the Word, so we do not give a false or inaccurate witness of God's message to human beings. "... *teaching them to observe all things that I have commanded you....,*" notice He doesn't say the parts we like. No, he says *"all things."* Not sure about your memory, but I often forget key passages of scripture....so I constantly find myself referring to the Word. Know that anything of God, will be verified by scripture. Therefore, whatever you speak in spreading the Gospel, needs to be backed by the Word. Study the Word, etch it in your hearts, so that you can carry out this directive of our Father.

Often in our lives, we spread information to our loved ones. Most times that information is based on our beliefs. These conversations may be about great deals at a favorite store, our sports heroes, political views, raising children, favorite recipes, the preferred way of performing a task....etc. We have no problem backing our views, at times making long impassioned speeches to do as such. When is the last time we gave such an impassioned speech to our loved ones about our faith though? In life we can get caught up sometimes with the things of this world, and neglect our responsibility to spread the most important issue at hand. The topic of our salvation and our personal walks with God. ***"And since we have the same spirit of faith, according to what is written 'I believed and therefore I spoke.' we also believe and therefore speak"*** (2 Corinthians 4:13 NKJV) We need to be as adamant about testifying about our faith, as we are about the "great deal" we just found. We are quick to spread news of the "great promotion" we received at work, and all our other accomplishments. Yet how often do we spread to others the greatness of what God has done in our lives. ***"Every good and perfect gift is from above, and comes down from the Father of lights, with whom there is no variation or shadow of turning."*** (James 1:17 NKJV) That means that every time something wonderful happens in your life, it's an opportunity for you to spread the word of God, an opportunity for you to tell of His goodness and mercy in your own life. Give God the glory in all things. ***"...in everything give thanks; for this is the will of God in Christ Jesus for you."*** (1 Thessalonians 5:18 NKJV) Examine yourself, and see if you're keeping these directives that Jesus has commanded for our lives. By giving thanks to God for all you have accomplished, you are witnessing and spreading His word. If you truly believe that God is the source of all that is good in your life, speak about it let the whole world know.

Our hope as Christians is that everyone will come and accept Christ as their Lord and savior. Oh, how happy I am that someone witnessed to me. That someone took the time out to pray, and show me what God has in store for my life. As Christians, we know that Jesus is our perfect example of how to live. He came to earth and lived a perfect life in submission to the Father, for **US!** He was perfect; He had no need to prove his faithfulness or righteousness to the Father. He loved us so much though that He was compelled to fulfill God's Word, and cleanse us of our sins. His only motivation for doing this was so that **we** could be one with the Father again. ***"Him we preach, warning every man and teaching every man in all wisdom, that we may present every man perfect in Christ Jesus."*** (Colossians 1:28 NKJV) This passage in Colossians tells us that our motivation should be the same as Jesus'. The purpose of being a good Christian and spreading the Word is not so we are revered by our peers. No, the purpose is so another may receive the grace and eternal life we have been granted. ***"Heal the sick, cleanse the lepers, raise the dead, cast out demons. Freely you have received, freely give."*** (Matthew 10:8 NKJV) Freely the Gospel we received has healed us, cleansed us from our iniquities, raised us from the death we were doomed to because of sin, and cast out the demons in our lives. You were not charged anything for this, not a single penny. To show your gratefulness you should be more than willing to go and do the same for someone else.

Do it not for recognition, or for earthly rewards, but to please the Father.

Now that we've established why we should preach the Gospel, we need to realize the necessity of being properly prepared to carry out such a great task. ***"Preach the word! Be ready in season and out of season. Convince, rebuke, exhort, with all longsuffering and teaching. For the time will come when they will not endure sound doctrine, but according to their own desires, because they have itching ears, they will heap up for themselves teachers; and they will turn their ears from the truth, and be turned to fables. But you be watchful in all things, endure afflictions, do the work of an evangelist, fulfill your ministry."*** (2 Timothy 4:2-5 NKJV) These are the words Paul sent to his "son in the faith" Timothy. He is telling him to be prepared at all times to spread the Gospel. *"Convince, rebuke, exhort, with all longsuffering and teaching."* We must present the Word in all of its applications, so that people recognize its practical place in their lives. We, who are believers are well aware the Word speaks to different aspects of our lives, and know that it is applicable in all situations. Therefore, we should **use all situations** as an opportunity to teach the Word. Paul goes on to warn Timothy that a time will come when people will not listen to his teachings. The same is true for us today. You may only have one chance to introduce someone to the majesty of the Gospel. Yes my friends, your witness may be their **only** opportunity to find salvation. ***"Brethren, if***

anyone among you wanders from the truth, and someone turns him back, let him know that he who turns a sinner from the error of his way will save a soul from death and cover a multitude of sins." (James 5:19-20 NKJV) So it is important that when those opportunities arise, you be ready and fervently pursue them. ***"Awake to righteousness, and do not sin,; for some do not have the knowledge of God. I speak this to your shame."*** (1 Corinthians 1:34 NKJV) This passage once again tells us of our responsibility to spread God's word. If there is a person you know has never been exposed to the Gospel, and you don't expose them to it, then you are at fault. IF one is exposed, and chooses not to believe, then your hands are clean...and so is your conscious. How can we as Christians, go to our graves with a clean conscience if we haven't been proper witnesses? How can we even call ourselves Christians if we don't go out of our way to spread the Word of God as Christ did?

"For if I preach the gospel, I have nothing to boast of, for necessity is laid upon me; yes, woe is me if I do not preach the gospel!" (1 Corinthians 16:9 NKJV) I would just like to reiterate the point; we should spread the Gospel because it is our duty, not because <u>we</u> are "righteous" people, I don't feel there is enough emphasis on this in our churches today. There are too many Sunday Christians...not enough Monday Ministers and Wednesday Worship Warriors. Oh, it's easy to go to church and talk about the goodness of God while in fellowship with the saints. Yet, is that truly accomplishing God's mission for his earthly kingdom? We must, out of appreciation for the work God is doing (and continues to do) in our lives.....bring that message to others. You should feel **obligated** to do as such, when you look back on all He's brought you through. *"Those who are wise will shine like the brightness of the firmament, and those who turn many to righteousness like the stars forever and ever."* (Daniel 12:30 NKJV) Show your appreciation for Christ's sacrifice, by truly putting on the mind of Christ. Our purpose in this world is to carry on Jesus' mission of spreading the Gospel, by bringing all peoples to repentance and in to a relationship with our heavenly Father. The next time you find yourself speaking about your accomplishments, or the good things happening in your life....give praise to the One who made it all possible. Don't be ashamed to tell people that all in your life you owe to him. It's your duty, and......*IT'S THE GOD'S HONEST TRUTH!!!!*

BE BLESSED BE FAITHFUL

WAIT ON GOD

"Therefore I will look to the Lord; I will wait for the God of my salvation; My God will hear me."
(Micah 7:7 NKJV)

"Blessed is the man who trusts in the Lord, and whose hope is the Lord."
(Jeremiah 17:7 NKJV)

"But those who wait on the Lord shall renew their strength; they shall mount up with wings like eagles, they shall run and not be weary, they shall walk and not faint."
(Isaiah 40:31 NKJV)

"My soul, waits silently for God alone, for my expectation is from Him. He only is my rock and my salvation; He is my defense; I shall not be moved."
(Psalms 62:5-6)

"Be still, and know that I am God; I will be exalted among the nations, I will be exalted in the earth."
(Psalms 46:10 NKJV)

I've often been told that what we seek to teach others is usually a lesson most needed for self. That is surely the case with this subject. For it surely speaks to me in my own life, and I hope it is needed and speaks to yours. Let us learn together how to be patient, and wait on our Father to provide our needs. Personally I find this to be one of the bigger crosses to bear in my own life. I am a highly motivated person, and dare I say....highly independent. Therefore when situations occur, I most often feel as though I can fix it. I have a million ways to rationalize why "I can handle it." One of my favorites is, "God helps those who help themselves." Anybody else hide behind that one....c'mon, I know I'm not alone. LOL Allow me to inform those of you who are unaware that phrase is nowhere in the Bible. Break out your concordances, consult your Pastors....let me know when you find it, because I'm looking for it. With that said, how many of us have lived our lives by this little saying? Hmmmmm? How much time have we spent depending on self to get something done, that only He can accomplish?

Adults, children, all of mankind suffer from the same issue, .the want for instant gratification. When we want something, we want it right now. Whether it's good or bad for us, productive or self-destructive. With no regard for the consequences. When we want it, we want it. ...no time for delay. Many of us "adults" are nothing more than toddlers with beards, bank accounts, and soccer games to get to. We go to God in prayer and expect him to say

"VOILA!!!" Problem solved. Sadly, often times that is not the result we receive. And because of our skewed expectations, our faith goes through some serious trials. ***"Therefore I will look to the Lord; I will wait for the God of my salvation; My God will hear me."*** (Micah 7:7 NKJV) Notice the key word Micah uses in this passage....**WAIT!** If you truly trust in God, and recognize who He really is, .what gives you the right to put Him on a time schedule? What type of trust do you display when you second guess Him? None at all, and as it says in James; ***"For not let that man suppose that he will receive anything from the Lord; he is a double-minded man, unstable in all his ways."*** (James 1:7-8) Does that answer why you're still waiting on a response for your prayer? The last part of the passage from Micah is... "My God will hear me." Micah knew and trusted in the Father, he didn't second guess. Notice there is a period and not a question mark, that means He made a statement. We must be the same in our life when God puts us in a "holding pattern." Hold on to the many times in your life when He has pulled you through. Meditate on the times you thought "it" was over, and in actuality "it" was just a new beginning. We never know what God truly has planned, so we must trust...and patiently wait on Him.

Let's move on to our next passage of scripture. ***"Blessed is the man who trusts in the Lord, and whose hope is the Lord."*** (Jeremiah 17:7 NKJV) Blessed, isn't that what we're all hoping to receive? Isn't that the purpose of all of our prayers in one way or another? Aren't we essentially asking God to bless our families, jobs, homes, circumstances, friendships....the list goes on and on. One definition of trust is..."hopeful reliance on what will happen in the **future**." The key word in that definition is future. That means something to come, yet not in the present. So we must, you guessed it, wait. Whenever we decide to take on a task we have asked God to take care of, we are blatantly saying we don't trust in Him to handle it for us. We have decided to place more trust in self, then in the Supreme Creator. Is this to say that God will not tell us to put forth effort to accomplish our goals? Of course not, what you have to ask yourself is, are you telling yourself to move forward or is God telling you to move forward? More often than not, you'll find it's you and not God. That is why the goal is never accomplished, or the results you're hoping for are only temporary. ***"It is better to trust in the Lord than to put confidence in man."*** (Psalm 118:8 NKJV) That would be any man, including self. Put your trust in God. Be patient, hopeful, and faithful.

    We all have friends who live in submission to God. No matter what circumstance comes their way in life, they place their hope and trust in the Father....and always seem to come out on top. That is because God is well pleased with them, and they have found the key to what life **is** all about. There is nothing we can do for self better than He can do for us. Sure, we can go and do what we feel should be done. After a lot of hard work, and hours wasted bumping our head, we just might get it done. Yet if we let God handle it we could save a boatload of sweat, pain, and time. ***"But those who wait on the Lord shall renew their strength; they shall mount up with wings like eagles, they shall run and not be weary, they shall walk and not faint."*** (Isaiah 40:31 NKJV) We know that God is the source of all our strength. So we know that if we place Him in all that we do, He will provide everything needed to accomplish our task. Thus we will be rejuvenated. I don't know about you, but whenever I accomplish a goal I always have whole lot of energy. I feel like I can fly... run for miles...and all of a sudden I'm anything but tired. Now compare that to how you feel when you fall short of a goal. Yes, you may still be encouraged. You may even feel as though the next time you try "it," you'll do "it" without a flaw. More than likely though, you feel a sense of disappointment. You may even be bitter for a number of different reasons. Lastly, you may be dismayed and it may carry over into your next venture. Why go through all of that pain and let down if you don't have to? Why not learn some patience, and appreciate the effortless way God gets it done. He wants to help, He doesn't want you to do it by yourself. Isn't that the way any good Father would be?

    As a Christian, we know that God has set the standards by which we live. Standards which we can never meet on our own, so why do we attempt to? I am learning, as I hope many of you are, to just leave it in God's hands. Everything. Even the things I think

I have under control. Why you ask? I look back over my life and take inventory of all the times I've messed something up thinking I "have it -under control." I suggest you all do the same. ***"My soul, waits silently for God alone, for my expectation is from Him. He only is my rock and my salvation; He is my defense; I shalt not be moved."*** (Psalms 62:5-6) Make the decision in your life today to etch this scripture on your heart. **Do not move** for anyone or anything, but God. Place all your expectations on Him. The definition of expectation is...." a confident belief or strong hope that a particular event will happen." All that you hope or believe in should be based on our heavenly Father, not any other circumstance on earth. He is the one who gave His Son, so you could have eternal life. He is the one who has made a way out of no way every time you've felt like the walls were closing in. He's the one you've run to every time things were looking hopeless. He has never let you down, has He? Take that faith and apply it in all situations in life. Tell yourself that if God wants me to wait, then waiting is what I will do. Nothing anyone or anything can do should be able to change your mind. Oh, remember that song in times of distress...."He may not come when you want Him too, but He'll be there right on time; He's an on time God.....yes He is!"

"Be still, and know that I am God; I will be exalted among the nations, I will be exalted in the earth." (Psalms 46:10 NKJV) The first two words of this text are what we want to focus on; "Be still." He

Job 32:18

didn't say go do anything, just be still. See, if we ask God to do something He's going to take care of it. He's a jealous God, He wants the glory in all things. He doesn't need you to do anything! He created the entire universe in a matter of moments, most of us can't even seem to be on time to work from day to day. What in your human mind makes you think He needs you? Who has inflated your ego to the point that you feel you should have a share in His glory. *"Be still, and know that I am God..."* He's not just saying that to you, or for you. He's saying that so the whole world will know that it is He who has accomplished this task. Stand back and let Him have his way in your life, your finances, your relationships, in **EVERYTHING!!!!!** He has been telling humans to stand back and let Him handle things since the beginning of time. *"And Moses said to the people,* ***"Do not be afraid. Stand still, and see the salvation of the Lord, which He will accomplish for you today. For the Egyptians whom you see today, you shall see again no more forever. The Lord will fight for you, and you shall hold your peace."*** (Exodus 14:13-14 NKJV) If he parted the Red Sea for the children of Israel, what makes you think He won't take care of that promotion for you? If He fed them manna for 40 years in the wilderness, what makes you think He can't make sure you're fed? Oh, if you would just wait on the Lord....what magnificent things He has in store for you. Get out of His way, and watch the blessings flow. Let Him get the glory, because He deserves it.

Pray for me, that I may learn patience and how to wait on the Lord. I'll be praying for you. In fact let's just pray for mankind as a whole. That instead of trying to figure out how to fix all of society's ills, we just let God take care of it. Trust in His word, trust in His power…..trust in His **_LOVE_**. What could be better to wait for?

<u>BE BLESSED BE FAITHFUL</u>

Job 32:18

"Lord God bless me with the faith of Abraham, the humility of Moses, the zeal of Jacob and Phinehas, the fearlessness of Joshua and Caleb, the heart of David, the wisdom of Solomon, the favor of Daniel and Joseph, the boldness of Stephen, the obedience of angels, and the anointing of Jesus." AMEN

Dear Danielle   March 24, 2010

    Hello, and how are you doing? I pray this letter reaches you in good health and wonderful spirits. It took me about 4 and a half months to write this letter. I've finally learned to put sincere thought behind my words, and bigger than that, let the spirit guide me. I prayed long and hard if I should even write this letter, if it would do more damage than good. The purpose of this letter is to express my love and fear of the Lord. Love for the blessings, mighty works, mercy and grace He has shown and continues to show in my life. Love for the purpose and will He is revealing for my life. I truly fear being outside of His will, and the repercussions of doing so. Bear with me, with His guidance; I'll do my best to show how this involves you.

    Philippians 1:3 (NIV) reads, "**I thank my God every time I remember you;**" and James 1:16-17 (NIV) reads... "**Don't be deceived, my dear brothers. Every good and perfect gift is from above, coming down from the Father of the heavenly lights, who does not change like shifting shadows.**" You have been good and perfect in my life, a blessing in the highest degree. In ways I didn't know before, and that may even surprise you. Galatians 1:10 (NIV) reads, "**Am I now trying to win the approval of men, or of God? Or am I trying to please men, I would not** be a servant of Christ." 1 John 4:5-6 reads, "**You, dear children, are from God and have overcome them, because the one who is in you is greater than the one who is in the world.. They are from the world and therefore speak from the viewpoint of the world, and the world listens to them. We are from God, and whoever knows God listens to us; but whoever is not from God does not listen to us. This is how we recognize the Spirit of truth and the spirit of falsehood.**" Those two passages explain the whole, "Danielle and Adryann" thing. The reason why no one understands our connection and it can't be put in to words... that's the way He intended it to be.

Another thing I've come to terms with is... I am dumb. Not an idiot, just too intelligent, I over think things. 1 Corinthians 8:2-3 (NIV) says, "**The man who thinks he knows something does not yet know as he ought to know. But the man who loves God is known by God.**" Now I understand why you always called me dumb, and 1 Corinthians 8:1 describes why you were doing that..." **We know that we all possess knowledge. Knowledge puffs up, but <u>love</u> builds up.**" You weren't trying to insult me or tear me down, you were teaching me humility to build me up. Please don't take the next passage out of context Layne, it will make perfect sense. 1 Peter 3:1-4 (NIV) says, "**Wives, in the same way be submissive to your husbands so that, if any of** them do not believe the word, they may be won over without words by the behavior of their wives, when they see the purity and reverence of your lives. Your beauty should not come from outward adornment, such as braided hair and the wearing of gold jewelry and fine clothes. Instead, it should be that of your inner self, the unfading beauty of a gentle and quiet spirit, which is of great worth in God's sight."** Simply put you have always led by example… me listening was the issue. This also illustrates why you never tripped off the material things. Danielle, if I never said it, <u>**I've always loved you…the real inner you**</u>. I apologize if I ever showed anything other than that. As far as me being the "lookout king," Proverbs 19:4, 6-7 reads, **"Wealth brings many friends, but a poor man's friend deserts him."** , **"Many curry favor with a ruler, and everyone is the friend of a man who gives gifts. A poor man is shunned by all his relatives – how much more do his friends avoid him! Though he pursues them with pleading, they are nowhere to be found."** LOL, yeah… you're <u>always</u> right. Child of the King… and He speaks through you.

    Now this is the part that makes me want to listen, adore, provide, and <u>never </u>be estranged from you. I remember back on Astoria how "disgusted" you would be with me every time I contemplated running my own "business" I didn't understand

Job 32:18

why you were so adamant. Beyond the fact I'm in jail (b/c that could have been avoided by listening to you), these passages that follow… show the root of your belief against me "working". Romans 12:1 (NIV) reads, **"For although they knew God, they neither glorified Him as God nor gave thanks to Him, but their thinking became <u>futile and their foolish</u> hearts were darkened."** WOW! Now I see what you were seeing, I'm ashamed, the next passage explains how I must've looked to you trying to justify it. Romans 1:28 – 32 (NIV) **"Furthermore since they did not think it worthwhile to retain the knowledge of God, He gave them over to a debased mind, to do what ought to not be done. They have become filled with every kind of wickedness, evil, greed, and depravity. They are full of envy, murder, strife, deceit, and they <u>invent</u> ways of doing evil; they disobey their parents; they are <u>senseless, faithless, heartless, ruthless</u>. Although they know God's righteous decree that those who do such things deserve death, <u>they not only continue to do these very things but also approve of those who practice them</u>."** No wonder you kicked me out of your life for all that time.

    Yet after all that; God placed a spirit in you that allowed me back in. I was determined not to be a burden, **"Like a bad tooth or lame fool is reliance on the unfaithful in times of trouble."**

(Proverbs 25:19 NIV) So I backslid in to my own business. Dumb move, figured I should know better. "**Better a little with the fear of the Lord than great wealth with turmoil. Better a meal of vegetables were there is love then a fattened calf with hatred.**" (Proverbs 15:16-17 NIV)

Going nowhere fast, and begging you to turn a blind eye. You always knew. From the very beginning, that's why didn't like my friends. "**A man who strays from the path of understanding comes to rest in the company of the dead.**" (Proverbs 21:16 NIV) Thought I had it all figured out, but... "**There is no wisdom, no insight, no plan that can succeed against the Lord.**" (Proverbs 21:30 NIV) He has a plan for me, I kept denying it... look where I'm at. He gets His way. Ironic part... who was always telling me to fear the Lord? That's why I love you. As far as when I would say everything I do fails when we're at odds, "**The house of the wicked will be destroyed, but the tent of the upright will flourish.**" (Proverbs 14:11 NIV) Not implying I was wicked, but that which fueled me was. Now when I'm with you, "**By wisdom a house is built, and through understanding it is established; through knowledge it's rooms are filled with rare and beautiful treasures.**" (Proverbs 24:34 NIV) A good woman brings wisdom, you're an extraordinary woman... words don't describe your significance.

Job 32:18

The letter I wrote you last year when all this happened said sometimes bad things have to happen, for the best things to come. My faith was in self and man, I wasn't paying God his due respect so He started to remove the people I loved most. Refer to Romans 1:28; first me and you fall out, then Pops dies, then Karl gets knocked. See, He wanted to test if me recommitting to His will was real. The cherry on top was turning myself in October 14, 2009. Faith and obedience must be wholehearted, and to be a man of God I must deal with the consequences of my actions. Galatians 6:7 (NIV) reads, **"Do not be deceived: God cannot be mocked. A man reaps what he sows."** Proverbs 14:14 (NIV) then states, **"The faithless will be fully repaid for their ways, and the good man rewarded for his."**

So this time of incarceration, is actually a time of preparation. James 1:2-4 (NIV) says, **"Consider it pure joy, my brothers, whenever you face trials of many kinds, because you know that the testing of your faith develops perseverance. Perseverance must finish its work so that you may be mature and complete, not lacking anything."** James 1:12 (NIV) says, **"Blessed is the man who perseveres under trial, because when he has stood the test, <u>he will receive the crown of life that God has promised to those who love Him</u>."** I want that crown Lady D, more than anything in this whole wide world.

Remember I used to say when it was time I'd be a preacher... that time is here. I've written dozens of sermons, and I don't know how many bible studies. I was helping with the youth group at the church before I turned myself in. More about that later.

"In the way of righteousness there is life; along that path is immortality." (Proverbs 12:28 NIV) **"A good name is more desirable than great riches; to be esteemed is better than silver and gold.**" (Proverbs 22:1 NIV) These passages along with Philippians 4:8, guide me daily. Though I've been running from His calling for my life, I'm appreciative He still has a work for me to do. "...**so is my word that goes out from my mouth: It will not return to me empty, but will accomplish what I desire and achieve the purpose for which I sent it.**" (Isaiah 55:11 NIV)

When I turned myself in after I came to get my clothes, I prayed God would show me a different way. So... there's a non-profit named C.H.O.I.C.E.S. he has put on my heart. It's for youth, sort of like a super-charged Y.M.C.A. / Big brothers, Big Sisters. There's another non-profit I'm still planning called Frontline Faith, it'll be an inter-faith community outreach program. Lastly, there's Mustard Seed Ministry. It'll be a venue to distribute sermons, bible studies, and other materials He has placed on my heart. Jeremiah 29:11 (NIV) states, **"For I know the plans I have for you, plans to give you hope and a future."**

Divine direction, and three companies while I'm incarcerated; why didn't I do His will before? I can hear you... "Because you're dumb UgMug."

No one knows me like you Danielle. I can out talk, and out think most anything breathing... except Danielle Renee. LOL!! 1 Samuel 16:7 (NIV) puts it, ".... **Man looks at the outward appearance, but the Lord looks at the heart**." That's how you've always dealt with me. No matter if I had money and was fresh to death you'd tell me to get it together. When I'm down and out... with everyone against me, you're still in my corner. UgMug or Adryann... you always see the real me. How could I have been so blind? "Because you're dumb UgMug," said Danielle. LOL.

There's no way to rectify the past, only God and time can do that. All I can do is to continue walking the path He's laid, and valuing all He's done in my life. My relationship with you is a HUGE portion of that Danielle. As I said in the beginning, you have been a blessing in the highest degree and, "**Through love and faithfulness sin is atoned for; through the fear of the Lord a man avoids evil**." (Proverbs 16:7 NIV) See how it all ties in; love and fear for God... with you? Bear with me a little longer. "**And so we know and rely on the love God has for us. God is love. Whoever lives in love lives in God, and God in him. In this way, love is made complete among us so that we will have confidence on the day of** judgment, because in this world <u>we</u> are like Him. There is no fear in love. <u>**But perfect love drives out fear, because fear has to do with punishment.**</u> **The one who fears is not made perfect in love.**" I'm not crazy for loving you Danielle, now I realize that more than ever. I see how God has worked through you to me, I see Him in you, now there are two reasons why I truly love you.

"**Love is patient, love is kind. It does not envy, it does not boast, it is not proud. It is not rude, it is not self-seeking, it is not easily angered, it keeps no records of wrongs. Love does not delight in evil but rejoices with the truth.** <u>**It always protects, always trusts, always hopes, always perseveres. Love never fails**</u>**. But where there are prophecies, they will cease; where there are tongues, they will be stilled; where there is knowledge, it will pass away.**" "**And now these three remain: faith, hope, and love. But the greatest of these is love.**" (1 Corinthians 13:4-8,13) Now that I know the love you deserve, are entitled to, and is required… things are much clearer. Loving and appreciating you doesn't just appease you… it glorifies Him. Yes, the dummy finally gets it. Every time I've ever wronged you, I wronged the Father and you. Leave it to me to be moving so fast, I don't see the implications of my actions. "**Hatred stirs up dissensions, but love covers all wrongs.**" (Proverbs 10:12 NIV)

Job 32:18

Another lesson I've learned is the difference between asking for forgiveness, and repentance. I'm sure you already know, but just in case I'll give a brief summation. Forgiveness is an act of the offended party. Repentances is an act of the offender to turn away, <u>and not to repeat the same offenses</u>. That hit me like a ton of shame. All the times you forgave me, not once did I repent. Not once did I go to the Father and ask for His power and strength to fill my weaknesses… that's why I was a repeat offender. There's a word in the middle of sin… I… Self-sufficiency is over rated, only God has the power to change us and control us… if we strive to live a **<u>righteous</u>** life.

"And we know that in all things God works for the good of those who love Him, who have been called according to His purpose." (Romans 8:28 NIV) I'm not asking you to take me back, or everything to be how it was. One, because that would be foolish…and a fool you are not. Insanity is basically doing the same thing, expecting a different result, and you're not insane. Two, you can't take back that person, because that person no longer exists. I'm asking if you will be willing to get to know the new creature He's called me to be. I'll be here until June 2011, plus whatever time Prince William gives me. I'll warn you, I'm a bit of a nerd… but Him in me has improved my personality. =) Not trying to preach to you, it's clear you minister to me, just want you to know the real me.

I prayed hard to God, to take it off my heart if being with you would be against His will. The results have been dreams of our good times, and scriptures that lead me back to you. "**There is surely a future hope for you, and your hope will not be cut off.**" (Proverbs 23:18 NIV) I know there's been terrible times, and I can't begin to apologize. I do know, "**I will repay you for the years the locusts have eaten – the great locust and the young locust, the other locusts and the locust swarm – my great army that I sent among you.**" (Joel 2:25 NIV) That means God can give back the time I fouled up, the next verse says,"… **You will have plenty to eat, until you are full, and you will praise the name of the Lord your God, who has worked bold wonders for you, never again will my people be ashamed**." (Joel 2:26 NIV) Things will get better Danielle, better than we could ever imagine.

There's a lot more, but this is what He has put on my heart up to now to reveal. Everything He's prepared has you written all over it. The purpose of this letter. is to express my love & fear of God. My life with Him as the Head; and my desire to show appreciation for the most precious blessing He's bestowed upon me. Your place is paramount, and permanent in my life. My better half… literally, & now He's the other half. A life of servitude to the Father, and the Love He's blessed me with. Sounds like what being a Christian is all about. He's made a way for us to reconcile, and I knkow it won't be a snap process. Just wondering if we could get started. **"Not that I have already obtained all this, or have already been made perfect, but I press on to take hold of that for which Christ Jesus took hold of me. Brothers, I do not consider myself yet to have taken hold of it. <u>But one thing I do: Forgetting what is behind and straining toward what is ahead</u>, I press on toward the goal to win the prize for which God has called me heavenward in Christ Jesus."** (Philippians 3:12-14 NIV) **"He who pursues righteousness and love, finds life, prosperity and honor."** (Philippians 21:21 NIV)

With that said, my prayers are with you. Give my love to all. You spoiling that nephew of yours? Ms. Tina loves being Grandma, don't she? How's Britt Brat? Your grandfolks? How about you, you've been on my heart lately. You OK?

Be Blessed Be Faithful,

Adryann M. Glenn (Ecclesiastes 4:13-14)

Contact Info
www.EMStreetbooks.com
adryann.glenn@gmail.com
mustardseedva.weebly.com
www.facebook.com/adryann.glenn.1

www.ingramcontent.com/pod-product-compliance
Lightning Source LLC
Chambersburg PA
CBHW020904090426
42736CB00008B/485